MAKING SENSE OF
MATHEMATICS
FOR TEACHING

Grades K–2

JULI K. DIXON

EDWARD C. NOLAN

THOMASENIA LOTT ADAMS

LISA A. BROOKS

TASHANA D. HOWSE

Solution Tree | Press

a division of

Solution Tree

555 North Morton Street
Bloomington, IN 47404
800.733.6786 (toll free) / 812.336.7700
FAX: 812.336.7790

email: info@solution-tree.com
solution-tree.com

Visit **go.solution-tree.com/mathematics** to download the free reproducibles in this book.

Printed in the United States of America

20   19   18   17   16   1   2   3   4   5

Library of Congress Control Number: 2016931406

ISBN: 978-1-942496-39-7

Solution Tree
Jeffrey C. Jones, CEO
Edmund M. Ackerman, President

Solution Tree Press
President: Douglas M. Rife
Senior Acquisitions Editor: Amy Rubenstein
Managing Production Editor: Caroline Weiss
Senior Production Editor: Rachel Rosolina
Proofreader: Ashante K. Thomas
Text and Cover Designer: Abigail Bowen

Acknowledgments

My deepest love and gratitude to my daughters, Alex and Jessica, who continue to allow me to understand mathematics more deeply through their eyes, and to my husband, Marc, who supports me to spend countless hours doing so. Thanks to Rachel Rosolina for her expertise and flexibility in supporting us to make the best book possible. Finally, thanks to Jeff Jones, Douglas Rife, and Stefan Kohler from Solution Tree for believing and investing in our vision to make sense of mathematics for teaching.

—Juli Dixon

Many thanks to my family, Michele and Calvin, for the wonderful support they continue to provide me in all of my endeavors. I also wish to thank our wonderful team of authors—Juli, Thomasenia, Lisa, and Tashana—from whom I have learned so much in the writing of this book.

—Ed Nolan

I am most grateful for the presence of my husband, Larry, and our sons, Blake, Philip, and Kurt, in my life. Many others support me and my work, and they include my mother, T. R. Lott, my six siblings, my pastors, and many dear friends. I am also thankful for the Dixon Nolan Adams Mathematics associates for working as a collaborative team to refine the delivery of the contents of this book.

—Thomasenia Adams

To my amazing family, for all the love and support they give me; to my colleagues, who made this book possible; and to teachers everywhere, who are changing the world.

—Lisa Brooks

To Mark and Kenny—thank you for all your support and love.

—Tashana Howse

Solution Tree Press would like to thank the following reviewers:

Sharon Brown
First-Grade Teacher
Oliver Beach Elementary School
Baltimore, Maryland

Jennifer Johnson
First-Grade Teacher
Jefferson Elementary School
Des Moines, Iowa

Henry Kepner
Professor Emeritus, Curriculum and Instruction
University of Wisconsin-Milwaukee
Milwaukee, Wisconsin

Stephanie Luke
Mathematics and Science Visiting Instructor
University of Central Florida
Orlando, Florida

Samantha Neff
Mathematics Coach
Highlands Elementary School
Winter Springs, Florida

Helen Spruill
Mathematics Coach
PS 503, The School of Discovery
Brooklyn, New York

Taylar Wenzel
Lecturer in Elementary Education
University of Central Florida
Orlando, Florida

Visit **go.solution-tree.com/mathematics** to download the free reproducibles in this book.

Table of Contents

CHAPTER 5
Geometry

CHAPTER 6
Measurement

About the Authors

Juli K. Dixon, PhD, is a professor of mathematics education at the University of Central Florida (UCF) in Orlando. She coordinates the award-winning Lockheed Martin/UCF Academy for Mathematics and Science for the K–8 master of education program as well as the mathematics track of the doctoral program in education. Prior to joining the faculty at UCF, Dr. Dixon was a secondary mathematics educator at the University of Nevada, Las Vegas and a public school mathematics teacher in urban school settings at the elementary, middle, and secondary levels.

She is a prolific writer who has authored and coauthored books, textbooks, chapters, and articles. A sought-after speaker, Dr. Dixon has delivered keynotes and other presentations throughout the United States. She has served as chair of the National Council of Teachers of Mathematics Student Explorations in Mathematics Editorial Panel and as a board member for the Association of Mathematics Teacher Educators. At the state level, she has served on the board of directors for the Nevada Mathematics Council and is a past president of the Florida Association of Mathematics Teacher Educators.

Dr. Dixon received a bachelor's degree in mathematics and education from the State University of New York at Potsdam, a master's degree in mathematics education from Syracuse University, and a doctorate in curriculum and instruction with an emphasis in mathematics education from the University of Florida. Dr. Dixon is a leader in Dixon Nolan Adams Mathematics.

To learn more about Dr. Dixon's work supporting children with special needs, visit www.astrokeofluck.net or follow @thestrokeofluck on Twitter.

Edward C. Nolan is the preK–12 director of mathematics for Montgomery County Public Schools in Maryland. He has nineteen years of classroom experience in both middle and high schools and was department chair for fifteen years, all in Montgomery County. An active member of the National Council of Teachers of Mathematics (NCTM), he is currently the president of the Maryland Council of Supervisors of Mathematics. Nolan is also a consultant for Solution Tree as one of the leaders of Dixon Nolan Adams Mathematics, providing support for teachers and administrators on the rigorous standards for mathematics.

Nolan has been published in the *Banneker Banner*, a publication of the Maryland Council of Teachers of Mathematics, and *Mathematics Teaching in the Middle School*, an NCTM publication, and he has conducted professional development at the state, regional, and national level, including webinars for NCTM and TODOS: Mathematics for ALL. His research interests lie in helping students and teachers develop algebraic thinking and reasoning. In 2005, Nolan won the Presidential Award for Excellence in Mathematics and Science Teaching.

He is a graduate of the University of Maryland. He earned a master's degree in educational administration from Western Maryland College.

To learn more about Nolan's work, follow @ed_nolan on Twitter.

Thomasenia Lott Adams, PhD, is an associate dean and professor of mathematics education in the College of Education at the University of Florida. She has mentored many future teachers of mathematics and mathematics teacher educators, and has served as a mathematics coach for grades K–12. She is the author of an elementary mathematics text series, academic books, and numerous peer-reviewed journal articles. Dr. Adams is a presenter at U.S. conferences and for professional development in school settings, which often includes teaching mathematics. She is also a trained National School Reform Faculty Certified Critical Friends Group coach.

Dr. Adams previously served as editor for the Mathematical Roots Department in *Mathematics Teaching in the Middle School* and coeditor for the Investigations Department of *Teaching Children Mathematics.* She is a past board member for the Association of Mathematics Teacher Educators and School Science and Mathematics Association. She is also a past president of the Florida Association of Mathematics Teacher Educators and a recipient of the Mary L. Collins Teacher Educator of the Year Award from the Florida Association of Teacher Educators.

Dr. Adams has engaged in many high-impact mathematics education projects, including Algebra Nation, an online platform for supporting the teaching and learning of algebra. She was also the team leader for mathematics and science job-embedded professional development for middle and high school mathematics and science teachers. Dr. Adams is a leader in Dixon Nolan Adams Mathematics.

Dr. Adams received a bachelor of science in mathematics from South Carolina State College and a master of education and doctorate of philosophy in instruction and curriculum with an emphasis in mathematics education from the University of Florida.

To learn more about Dr. Adams's work, follow @TLAMath on Twitter.

Lisa A. Brooks, EdD, is a lecturer in the College of Education and Human Performance at the University of Central Florida. She teaches classes in mathematics and science education in the elementary education program. Her research is focused on helping teachers facilitate student discourse to increase conceptual understanding of mathematics. Dr. Brooks has been in the field of education since 1992. She has experience teaching elementary and middle school students. She was also the team leader for mathematics and science job-embedded professional development for middle and high school mathematics and science teachers.

Dr. Brooks is the recipient of a PRISM (Promoting Regional Improvement in Science and Math) Outstanding Mathematics Teacher Award. She is also a published author of multiple articles in state and national journals, as well as one in an international journal. She has experience presenting at state and national conferences for educators, school leaders, district leaders, and teacher educators.

Dr. Brooks received a bachelor's degree in elementary education from the University of Central Florida. She is a Lockheed Martin Scholar with a master's degree in K–8 mathematics and science education. She earned a doctorate in curriculum and instruction with a focus on mathematics education from the University of Central Florida. She is certified in elementary education, primary education, and English for Speakers of Other Languages (ESOL).

To learn more about Dr. Brooks's work, follow @DrBrooksla on Twitter.

 **Tashana D. Howse, PhD,** is an assistant professor of mathematics education at Daytona State College, where she teaches mathematics and science methods courses for elementary and secondary education majors. Her research focuses on teachers' use of culturally responsive teaching practices to support student engagement in Mathematical Practices defined within the Common Core State Standards.

Her mathematics teaching experience ranges from classroom public education to developing the teachers of tomorrow through preservice teacher education courses. She has been a secondary mathematics teacher and a mathematics instructor at Bethune-Cookman University.

Dr. Howse has presented at local, state, and national conferences. She has also participated in an African teacher exchange program, where she worked with Namibian teachers to enhance mathematics teaching. She has coauthored articles for journals published by NCTM and the Research Council on Mathematics Learning.

She earned her bachelor's and master's degrees in mathematics education from Florida State University and her doctorate of philosophy in mathematics education from the University of Central Florida.

To learn more about Dr. Howse's work, follow @tdhowse_math on Twitter.

To book Juli K. Dixon, Edward C. Nolan, Thomasenia Lott Adams, Lisa A. Brooks, or Tashana D. Howse for professional development, contact pd@solution-tree.com.

Introduction

The only way to learn mathematics is to do mathematics.

—Paul Halmos

When teaching, much of the day is spent supporting students to engage in learning new content. In mathematics, that often means planning for instruction, delivering the planned lessons, and engaging in the formative assessment process. There are opportunities to attend conferences and other professional development events, but those are typically focused on teaching strategies or on administrative tasks like learning the new gradebook program. Opportunities to take on the role of *learner* of the subject you teach are often not available. As you read *Making Sense of Mathematics for Teaching Grades K–2*, you will have the chance to become the learner once again. You will *learn* about the mathematics you teach by *doing* the mathematics you teach.

There is a strong call to build teachers' content knowledge for teaching mathematics. A lack of a "deep understanding of the content that [teachers] are expected to teach may inhibit their ability to teach meaningful, effective, and connected lesson sequences, regardless of the materials that they have available" (National Council of Teachers of Mathematics [NCTM], 2014, p. 71). This lack of deep understanding may have more to do with lack of exposure than anything else.

All too often, exposure to mathematics is limited to rules that have little meaning. Teachers then pass these rules on to students. For example, how mathematics is taught in kindergarten influences students' understanding of mathematics in later years. If a teacher says "addition always makes bigger" as a way to help young learners differentiate between addition and subtraction, this meaning for addition becomes worthless when students encounter adding negative numbers in middle school. The rule applies to problems like 3 + 2 where the sum is 5 but not for problems like –3 + –2 where the sum is –5, which is less than either addend. This is an example of what Karen S. Karp, Sarah B. Bush, and Barbara J. Dougherty (2014) refer to as *rules that expire*. Providing rules that work in the short term but cannot be applied in the long term are counterproductive to supporting students with meaningful school mathematics experiences. Teachers must attend to precision when teaching concepts in mathematics, or students will learn incorrect information. Students will need to later unlearn those misconceptions—and unlearning a concept can be more difficult than learning it correctly the first time. This happens when teachers are not afforded the opportunity to develop a deep understanding of the mathematics they teach.

This book is our response to requests from teachers, coaches, supervisors, and administrators who understand the need to know mathematics for teaching but who don't know how to reach a deeper level of content knowledge or to support others to do so. First and foremost, the book provides guidance for refining what it means to be a teacher of mathematics. To teach mathematics for depth means to facilitate instruction that empowers students to develop a deep understanding of mathematics. This can happen when teachers are equipped with strong mathematics content knowledge—knowledge that covers the conceptual and procedural understanding of mathematics and knowledge that is supported by a variety of strategies and tools for engaging students to learn mathematics. With these elements as a backdrop, this book can be used to go below the surface in core areas of mathematics.

Second, coaches, supervisors, and administrators benefit from the content and perspectives provided in this book because it offers a source that supports guidance and mentoring to enhance teachers' mathematics content knowledge and their knowledge for teaching mathematics. They can particularly benefit from this book as a resource for helping them recognize expected norms in mathematics classrooms.

Here, we will set the stage for what you will learn from this book along with the rationale for why it is important for you to learn it. First, we provide some of the reasons why teachers need to understand mathematics with depth. Next, we share the structure of each chapter along with a description of what you will experience through that structure. Finally, we present ways that you will be able to use this book as an individual or within a collaborative team.

A Call for Making Sense of Mathematics for Teaching

Often, teachers are not initially aware that they lack sufficient depth of mathematical understanding or that this depth of understanding is critical to being equipped to guide students' mathematical development. What we have found is that engaging in tasks designed to contrast procedural and conceptual solution processes provides a window into the gap left by teaching mathematics without understanding.

Procedural skill includes the ability to follow rules for operations with a focus on achieving a solution quickly, while *conceptual understanding* includes comprehension of mathematical ideas, operations, and relationships. The procedure for adding multidigit numbers with regrouping is one that most teachers can execute without much thought, yet the conceptual understanding needed to explain the process for regrouping based on place value might be less accessible. Thus, the contrast between typical solution processes and those that develop conceptual understanding highlights the need to truly know mathematics in order to teach it.

As a team, we provide large-scale professional development workshops for school districts across the United States and beyond. We often begin our presentations by engaging participants in a short mathematical activity to set the stage for the types of mind-shifting approaches necessary to teach for depth. One such activity explores an invented algorithm for adding multidigit numbers. In grade 2, students are asked to add multidigit numbers prior to learning the standard algorithm of lining up the addends vertically, adding the ones and regrouping if necessary, and then adding the tens. (This standard algorithm might be better named the U.S. standard algorithm because there are other algorithms standard to other countries. In this book, *standard algorithms* will refer to the most common U.S. standard algorithms unless otherwise noted.) Consider the start of an explanation from a student who was asked to add 57 + 38 prior to being taught the standard algorithm (see figure I.1).

How would you respond to this student? Perhaps you would ask the student to stop the process because you worry that the student is confusing the ones and the tens based on the second step provided in figure I.1. It certainly appears that this could be a mistake on the part of the student. Our workshop participants are often comfortable with the student's first step but are not so comfortable with the second step. They, too, worry that the student has confused the tens and ones and is adding 7 ones to 3 tens for a sum of 10 ones. We then show the last two steps so that the entire sequence looks like figure I.2.

Perhaps, like our participants, you were certain that the student was in error based on his or her first two steps. However, the student reaches the correct sum. How could this be? Eventually, participants see that when the student added 7 + 3, he or she was not confusing place values but was breaking up the 8 ones from the 38 into 3 ones and 5 ones so that the student could add 7 + 3 to make a ten.

We ask the participants what they would have done if one of their students had begun solving a problem like this in a similar way. Many participants admit they would stop the student at the second step, when adding 7 + 3, to caution him or her against confusing place values, not recognizing that the

> Solve: 57 + 38
>
> 50 + 30 = 80
>
> 7 + 3 = 10

Figure I.1: Student's first steps of an invented algorithm for a multidigit addition task.

> Solve: 57 + 38
>
> 50 + 30 = 80
>
> 7 + 3 = 10
>
> 80 + 10 = 90
>
> 90 + 5 = 95

Figure I.2: Student's invented algorithm for a multidigit addition task.

student was using an excellent strategy—that of making a ten. However, this make-a-ten strategy is not taught in grade 2. It is taught in grade 1. If grade 1 teachers don't see the value in this strategy for future work leading to adding with regrouping, they might not emphasize this important strategy. If grade 2 teachers don't realize their students have been taught this strategy, they might fail to capitalize on it.

Some teachers miss opportunities to reinforce the development of number sense. Perhaps they aren't as open to different strategies or do not expose students to a variety of student-invented algorithms. In order to avoid issues like the previous example, teachers must also understand how content is developed from one year to the next, use effective mathematics practices to build mathematical proficiency in all students, and incorporate tasks, questioning, and evidence into instruction.

Understanding Mathematics for Teaching

How does one develop number sense that progresses to the building of efficient algorithms? Even if *you* have this knowledge, how do you help your fellow teachers or the teachers you support develop the same? Questions such as these led us to create our mathematics-content-focused professional development institutes and the accompanying follow-up workshops, in which teachers implement new skills and strategies learned at the mathematics institutes. Conversations during the follow-up workshops provide evidence that teachers benefit from knowing the mathematics with depth, as do the students they serve. After all, discussing number concepts and skills within teacher teams is a powerful way to develop a deep understanding.

We begin each follow-up workshop with a discussion of what is going well at the participants' schools and what needs further attention. Their responses to both queries reaffirm our need to focus on teachers' pedagogical content knowledge. A typical response regarding what is going well includes a discussion about how teachers are now able to make connections between the topics they teach. For example, teachers begin to recognize commonalities between topics, such as number and geometry; they see the connection between representing a number in different ways and the orientation of shapes. For instance, the number 12 can be written as 10 + 2 or as 12 ones. In the same way, a triangle is still a triangle regardless of its orientation. Teachers report that, in past years, they taught these two content areas as separate topics, making no connections to the importance of flexible understanding across mathematics, as though the topics existed in silos, completely separate. They taught without coherence. With a deeper understanding of their content, however, they note that they are able to reinforce earlier topics and provide rich experiences as they make connections from one topic to the next. Similarly, coaches report that their deeper mathematics understanding is useful in helping teachers attend to these connections during planning and instruction and within the formative assessment process. The formative assessment process includes the challenging work of evaluating student understanding throughout the mathematics lesson and unit. Teachers need a deep understanding of the mathematics they teach to support a thoughtful process of making sense of student thinking and being confident to respond to students' needs whether those needs include filling gaps, addressing common errors, or advancing ideas beyond the scope of the lesson or unit.

Through the mathematics institutes and workshops, participants realize the need for additional professional development experiences, but providing this level of support can be challenging for schools and districts. This book is our response to this need. We've designed it to support stakeholders who want a review as well as to address additional topics. Our approach herein is informed by our extensive experience providing professional development throughout the United States as well as internationally and is supported by research on best practices for teaching and learning mathematics.

Engaging in the Mathematical Practices

As teachers of mathematics, our goal for all students should be mathematical proficiency, regardless of the standards used. One way to achieve mathematical proficiency is to "balance *how* to use mathematics with *why* the mathematics works" (National Council of Supervisors of Mathematics [NCSM], 2014, pp. 20–21, emphasis added). Mathematical proficiency involves unpacking the mathematics embedded within learning progressions, developing and implementing an assortment of strategies connected to mathematical topics and the real world, being able to explain and justify mathematical procedures, and interpreting and making sense of students' thinking (Ball, Thames, & Phelps, 2008). These processes are well described by the eight Standards for Mathematical Practice contained within the Common Core State Standards (CCSS) for mathematics (National Governors Association Center for Best Practices [NGA] & Council of Chief State School Officers [CCSSO], 2010).

1. Make sense of problems and persevere in solving them.
2. Reason abstractly and quantitatively.
3. Construct viable arguments and critique the reasoning of others.
4. Model with mathematics.
5. Use appropriate tools strategically.
6. Attend to precision.

7. Look for and make use of structure.

8. Look for and express regularity in repeated reasoning.

The Mathematical Practices describe the ways that mathematically proficient students solve problems and engage in learning mathematics. What does this mean for you and your students? Since the Mathematical Practices truly describe how *students* engage with the mathematics, your role becomes that of facilitator, supporting this engagement. Think about 7 + 8. If your goal of instruction is for students to apply the make-a-ten strategy, in what ways should the students engage with this task? If you want them to think of 7 as close to 10 and 8 as 3 + 5, then making sense of the structure of making tens and number pairs would be appropriate. Knowing that 7 is three away from 10 and that 8 can be decomposed into 3 + 5 supports using structure. This structure makes use of the associative property of addition, something that might be missed without an emphasis on Mathematical Practice 7, "Look for and make use of structure." How should teachers facilitate this sort of discussion with students so that the teachers are not doing all the telling (and thinking)? It requires instruction that acknowledges the value of students talking about mathematics and using mathematics to communicate their ideas.

When the mathematics content and the Mathematical Practices are addressed in tandem, students have the best opportunity to develop clarity about mathematics reasoning and what it means to do mathematics successfully.

Emphasizing the TQE Process

As part of the professional development material in this book, we include videos of K–2 classroom episodes (and occasionally grades extending from this grade band) in which students explore rich mathematical tasks. Classroom videos extending beyond K–2 provide the opportunity to highlight coherence across grades. For example, a video of students in grade 4 is included to highlight the importance of having students create word problems in K–2 to prepare them for authoring more complex problems in the intermediate grades. In presenting these videos, we emphasize three key aspects of the teacher's role— (1) tasks, (2) questioning, and (3) evidence—which make up what we call the *TQE process*.

Our emphasis on the TQE process helps define a classroom that develops mathematics as a focused, coherent, and rigorous subject. Thus, we uphold the following tenets.

- **Teachers with a deep understanding of the content they teach select *tasks* that provide students with the opportunity to engage in practices that support learning concepts before procedures; they know that for deep learning to take place, students need to understand the procedures they use.** Students who engage in mathematical tasks are also engaged in learning mathematics with understanding. Consider grade 1 students who are making sense of basic facts. The order of the presented facts is important to address a specific learning goal. For example, if the goal is for students to make sense of using doubles to find facts that are near doubles as a means to determine a fact other than by rote, students might be presented with facts like 6 + 6 and 6 + 7 then 8 + 8 and 8 + 9. Students would be directed to identify a pattern in the pairs of facts as a way to see the value in applying the doubles-plus-one strategy. Once students identify the pattern, they can be led to see why knowing doubles can help them find sums where the addends are near doubles. These students are making sense of patterns in computation as a way of determining basic facts. Thus, this scenario provides insight into a classroom where carefully selected tasks support deeper learning.

- **Teachers who have a deep understanding of the content they teach facilitate targeted and productive *questioning* strategies because they have a clear sense of how the content progresses within and across grades.** For instance, in the grade 1 example, teachers would facilitate discussions around strategies for adding basic facts that focus on the application of properties of operations, such as the associative property of addition when solving 6 + 7. Teacher questioning encourages students to use relational thinking strategies by thinking 6 + 6 and adding one more or 6 + 7 = 6 + (6 + 1) = (6 + 6) + 1. While students do not need to know they are applying the associative property of addition, teachers do need to know so they ask questions that facilitate understanding, which leads to success with multidigit addition in later grades.

- **Teachers who have a deep understanding of the content they teach use *evidence* gained from the formative assessment process to help them know where to linger in developing students' coherent understanding of mathematics.** In the grade 1 example, teachers would look for evidence that students know their doubles and are using them appropriately to make sense of other basic facts.

Throughout the book and the accompanying classroom videos, we share elements of the TQE process to help you as both a learner and a teacher of mathematics. In addition, we ask that you try to answer three targeted questions as you watch each video. These questions are as follows:

1. How does the teacher prompt the students to make sense of the problem?

2. How do the students engage in the task; what tools or strategies are the students using to model the task?

3. How does the teacher use questioning to engage students in thinking about their thought processes?

Next, we describe the structure of the book to help guide your reading.

The Structure of Making Sense

To address the mathematical content taught in the primary grades, each chapter focuses on a different overarching topic. For instance, chapter 1 covers number concepts and place value. Chapter 2 then explores word problem structures. Chapter 3 takes a look at addition and subtraction using counting strategies, and chapter 4 covers addition and subtraction using grouping strategies. Chapter 5 examines geometry, and chapter 6 closes with a focus on measurement. These topics represent the big ideas for the primary grades. Each chapter concludes with a series of questions to prompt reflection on the topic under discussion.

We end the book with an epilogue featuring next steps to help you and your team to make sense of mathematics for teaching and implement this important work in your school or district.

To further break down each overarching topic, each chapter shares a common structure: The Challenge, The Progression, The Mathematics, The Classroom, and The Response.

The Challenge

Each chapter begins with an opportunity for you to engage in an initial task connected to the chapter's big idea. We call this section The Challenge because this task might challenge your thinking. We encourage you to stop and engage with the task before reading further—to actually *do* the task. Throughout the book, we alert you to the need to stop and do tasks with a *do now* symbol (see figure I.3).

Figure I.3: *Do now* symbol.

The presentation of mathematical ideas in this book may be different from how you learned mathematics. Consider being asked to find as many different ways as you can to represent fourths on a geoboard where the entire geoboard is the whole (see figure I.4).

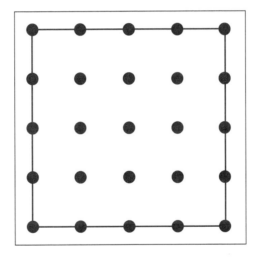

Figure I.4: A geoboard where the entire geoboard is the whole.

This task from chapter 6 may test your understanding of the mathematical topic being explored. For instance, you must justify how you know your examples differ from one another yet still represent fourths of the same whole, something you may not have considered in your own mathematics learning. Tasks in these sections focus on reasoning and sense making, since the rules of mathematics are developed through connections to earlier mathematical experiences rather than through procedures presented without meaning.

Since one purpose of this book is to engage you as a learner *and* teacher of mathematics, the tasks we ask you to explore support this goal. As a student of mathematics, you will consider how you learn mathematics. As a teacher of mathematics, you will explore how this newly found understanding could be the impetus for making sense of mathematics for teaching.

The Progression

Mathematics content knowledge is not enough. According to NCSM (2014), teachers must also *"understand how to best sequence, connect, and situate the content they are expected to teach within learning progressions"* (p. 24, emphasis in original). This means teachers need to know both the mathematics for their grade level and the mathematics that comes before and after their grade level—how the mathematics progresses over time.

Thus, each chapter highlights a progression of learning for a big idea. These progressions identify how learning develops over multiple years and highlight the importance of making sense of each building block along the way. The sequences defined by these progressions help the learner—and the teacher—make sense of the big idea in question. Understanding how content progresses provides avenues for supporting both the learner who struggles and the learner who needs enrichment.

Our placement of topics within grades was informed by the Common Core State Standards for mathematics (NGA & CCSSO, 2010). However, our discussion of how the mathematics is developed within the progressions was not limited by this interpretation. We do not refer to specific content standards from the Common Core in an effort to expand the discussion to include *all* rigorous mathematics standards, including those found outside of the United States. Note that because learning progressions develop over time, there will be occasions when this book addresses topics that reach into grades beyond grade 2.

The Mathematics

There is much talk about rigor in instruction these days, but what does *rigor* mean in the context of teaching and learning mathematics? A misnomer is that it means *hard* or *difficult*. Rather, *rigor* refers to the need to incorporate all forms of thinking about mathematics—including concepts, procedures, the language of mathematics, and applications—in the teaching and learning process. However, this raises several questions. What does this actually look like in instruction? What teacher actions expose all students to rigor? How do you balance rigor reflected by reasoning and sense making with the ability to recall addition facts?

Problems in a rigorous classroom build students' deep understanding of mathematics. Consider 7 + 8. You know the sum; you know it without needing to think. Yet what path do teachers use to bring students to this level? All too often, instruction begins and ends with memorization. Teachers use flash cards and games and spend time each day with practice, leaving some students able to recall the facts and some unable to recall the facts. Is this an example of teaching with rigor? The answer is no.

Importantly, rigor includes making sense of strategies based on properties of operations. Sense making should precede a focus on memorization, rules, and procedures. This is where teaching might get uncomfortable. You may not have been taught the strategies as a student or see the connections. Thus, within The Mathematics section in each chapter, you will unpack the big ideas so the mathematics is explicitly connected to ways of making this knowledge accessible and rigorous for your students. For example, if students use the doubles-minus-one strategy to find the sum of 7 + 8, what property have they used? Are they applying the associative property or the commutative property? The answer is both! Exploring mathematics in this way develops a deep personal understanding of mathematics. As you develop this understanding, procedures and algorithms will make sense, and you will be able to explain and justify them (NCTM, 2014). Through this process, we will support you in developing the knowledge to promote students' procedural fluency, which is defined as "skill in carrying out procedures flexibly, accurately, efficiently, and appropriately" (Kilpatrick, Swafford, & Findell, 2001, p. 116).

Many of the tasks throughout the book can be characterized as high-cognitive-demand tasks, which are "tasks that require students to think conceptually and that stimulate students to make connections that lead to a different set of opportunities for student thinking" (Stein & Smith, 1998, p. 269). Consideration for the understanding, creation, selection, and implementation of high-cognitive-demand tasks is vital for effective mathematics learning (Dixon, Adams, & Nolan, 2015). While including tasks that are high and low cognitive demand support a balance of conceptual understanding and procedural fluency, the cognitive demand of tasks often declines during instruction when the cognitive complexity of the task is not maintained (Kisa & Stein, 2015). How will you maintain the challenge of tasks through your actions? In this section and throughout the book, we provide you with excerpts from mathematics lessons so you can build a shared understanding of what mathematics instruction can look like in elementary class-rooms. In addition, we emphasize one or more of the best-aligned Mathematical Practices that support the learning of the relevant mathematics content. This is important regardless of whether you are teaching using the Common Core State Standards for mathematics. It describes good teaching and learning of any mathematical content.

The Classroom

In what ways do you support student learning in the mathematics classroom? For instance, do you encourage student discourse? Doing so allows you to consider what students are talking about and how you will respond to their talk. Your approach to student talk—and many other classroom aspects—helps determine the type of classroom learning community you and your students develop together. This class-room learning community is critical to the development of students' deep mathematical understanding.

The Classroom sections provide videos and extensive descriptions of what happens in engaging mathematics lessons. In order to assist you in thinking about how classrooms that develop mathematical understanding should look, each chapter includes two video episodes. These short videos show students exploring one task from the big idea of that chapter and one task from a related big idea. When you see the play button, please stop and watch the video. Included with the icon is the accompanying web address and a Quick Response (QR) code for you to access the video.

 www.solution-tree.com/Representing_Two-Digit_Numbers

We consider the accompanying videos to be further investment in our effort to support the teaching and learning of mathematics. You will have the opportunity to see the topics we write about in the book in action. For instance, when we discuss how to massage a task so that it engages students, elicits student talk, and uncovers students' errors, we then follow up by capturing the essence of these actions in real classrooms. This modeling of good mathematics teaching provides opportunities for teachers to discuss what is happening in their own classrooms with the same mathematics content. It is not always possible for teachers to leave the classroom to observe a fellow teacher engaged in mathematics instruction. Thus, these videos help fill this gap and also provide a context for teachers to try an approach to mathematics teaching as modeled in the videos.

You must also consider the classroom expectations set for students. For instance, what are the rules for students answering questions? These rules should be established and made explicit for students so they know what you expect of them when they work on tasks. Also, how do students work together on tasks? Students can benefit greatly from collaborative experiences in mathematics, but they need to know how to best collaborate with each other. In many instances, the student who is confident and right most of the time does most of the talking. Thus, helping students monitor and regulate their discourse is valuable for the mathematics learning experience. As illustrated in the classroom videos, we encourage three classroom norms for every mathematics classroom.

1. Explain and justify solutions.

2. Make sense of each other's solutions.

3. Say when you don't understand or when you don't agree.

The classroom norms need to support the active thinking of students rather than solely relying on the thinking of teachers, as is so often the case in teacher-centered classrooms. This point is true when students work on their own as well as when students work together. You should always provide students the opportunity to share their strategies and make sense of the thinking of other students in order to be sure they understand mathematics with depth.

The structure of the classroom needs to support the thinking and learning of the students, and different tasks may require different structures. Some tasks may include questions that help students make connections; other tasks may not need such support. One model that is often discussed in many schools and districts is the gradual release of responsibility, commonly described as the teaching practice where the teacher models ("I do"), then the class practices together ("We do"), and finally the students practice independently ("You do") (Fisher & Frey, 2003). Although this method is appropriate at times, we advocate for methods that include focus on the students making sense of and reasoning with mathematics. An alternative approach for mathematics is what we call *layers of facilitation*.

1. *I facilitate the whole class* to engage in meaningful tasks through questioning.

2. *I facilitate small groups* to extend the learning initiated in the whole-group setting.

3. *I facilitate individuals* to provide evidence of their understanding of the learning goal.

This change in teacher role focuses on the teacher as facilitator of knowledge acquisition rather than as a transmitter of knowledge. As you read the text and as you watch the videos, you will notice our focus is largely on implementing layers of facilitation, but it is important to recognize that there are some topics and mathematical content that need to be taught following the gradual release of responsibility model. It is important for you, as the teacher, to determine when to apply this model. Keep in mind that students will benefit from opportunities to have a more participatory role during instruction whenever possible.

The Response

How do you respond when students struggle? What do you do when students express misconceptions? It is important to use student errors as springboards for learning; the errors and the gaps in prerequisite knowledge that lead to those errors inform your everyday instruction as well as your response to intervention (RTI) process within a Multi-Tiered System of Supports (MTSS).

Again, consider how students approach 7 + 8. Perhaps they use their recall of the fact, or maybe they need to use other strategies to determine the sum. Think about questions you could ask in order to gather information about students' thinking processes, both when they have the correct answer as well as when they do not. When your students answer 18, how can you help them examine their thinking and correct their mistake without simply giving them the correct answer? One approach would be to ask questions to support the efforts of your students and encourage them to think of errors as beneficial in order to learn mathematics with depth. This is an area where your own depth of mathematical understanding is critical to help your students develop their thinking.

It is essential to explore your students' reasoning and sense making and break down that thinking in order to rebuild their understanding of mathematics. Effective teachers understand what models and strategies best support students in ways that allow them to connect their current thinking with the learning goal of the task. You can then use the evidence of the level of students' understanding you gather to inform your response both during and after instruction.

Now that you understand what is to come in the following pages, here's how we suggest you approach the book.

How to Use This Book

Collaborative teams of teachers can use this book to explore mathematics content and engage in discussions about teacher actions that will help bring mathematics to life for students. In fact, the entire TQE process is best accomplished by a collaborative team that works together to address the four critical questions—the guiding force of the professional learning community (PLC) culture (DuFour, DuFour, Eaker, & Many, 2010).

1. What do we want students to learn and be able to do?

2. How will we know if they know it?

3. How will we respond if they don't know it?

4. How will we respond if they do know it?

This book is an optimal tool for your collaborative team in a PLC culture. Although it is grade-band specific, it also provides support for vertical (across grades) discussions and planning. There are many topics in this book that can be addressed in your grade-level team or in your vertical team, including the Mathematical Practices. While the Mathematical Practices are not grade specific, how students engage with them can be expected to vary from grade to grade, and you can benefit from grade-specific as well as vertical discussions about them.

Our expectation is that individuals or collaborative teams will be able to use this book by reading the chapters in order. Within each chapter, we help you develop clarity about the mathematical content and its progression. Teachers often have questions about the sequence of mathematics content in mathematics texts and other resources—sometimes the sequence is aligned with authentic progressions and sometimes not. Thus, you can use this book as a resource to understand how background and underlying knowledge of mathematics support further understanding and how to best align mathematics curriculum with the progression of the content.

We hope this book and the accompanying videos will be your go-to source for a deep dive into relevant mathematics content, effective pedagogical actions, appropriate classroom norms, meaningful assessment, and collaborative teacher team efforts. Our goal is for this resource to connect the good work of mathematics teaching that you are already facilitating with the goals of improving mathematics teaching that you aspire to attain.

CHAPTER 1

Number Concepts and Place Value

Number concepts and place value provide the mathematical foundation that all students need for future success in mathematics. *Number concepts* describe the meaning of numbers and are prerequisite to making sense of operations (addition and subtraction and eventually multiplication and division). *Place value* involves how numbers are grouped in ones, tens, hundreds, and so on. As you consider these two pillars of mathematics, you will have the opportunity to think about ways in which students develop number sense and build an understanding of place value relationships. You will also learn about student misconceptions, how to facilitate student engagement through meaningful tasks, and ways to address common student errors related to number and place value.

There are several tools that help engage students with meaningful contexts to support their learning of these two concepts. We share these tools throughout the chapter. As you read, it is important to remember that students require time to make sense of number and place value. They benefit from being exposed to a variety of tasks that are conceptually based, grounded in everyday life experiences, and challenging to their present notions about number and place value.

The Challenge

In order to experience mathematics as a learner, we've provided a task for you to explore (see figure 1.1). The task is based on a context meaningful to students in developing an understanding of place value. Be sure to engage with the task prior to reading the remainder of the chapter.

Mr. and Mrs. Baylor own a candy shop. In this candy shop, candy is sold and packaged in a particular way. Candy is packaged as individual pieces. Candy is also packaged in rolls. Within each roll, there are 10 individual pieces of candy. Rolls are packaged in boxes. Each box contains 10 rolls. Mrs. Baylor put 347 candies on a shelf. How could the candies have been packaged? Show at least three different ways.

Figure 1.1: Candy packaging task.

How did you go about solving this problem? Maybe you used manipulatives, drew a picture, or used a mental image with numbers. You may have also begun with individual pieces or thought in terms of boxes or rolls first. Did you have a systematic way of approaching the problem or of representing your response? If you did, maybe your students would approach the problem differently. Think about the problems they might encounter or questions they might have about the candy shop context.

Packaging 347 candies in different ways is a meaningful experience because it sets the stage for you to recognize the ten-to-one relationship of the pieces, rolls, and boxes of candy. When you unpack a box to represent rolls, you have to remember that the box contains ten rolls. The structure of how the candy is packaged matches the structure of the base ten number system. This is an example of using Mathematical Practice 7, "Look for and make use of structure." In this case, the structure is the ten-to-one relationship of pieces to rolls and rolls to boxes and relating that understanding to place value. How would your students approach this task? What difficulties might they encounter? Later in this chapter, you will have the opportunity to watch a video of students using the candy shop model to build a conceptual understanding of place value.

It is beneficial for students to use the candy shop model to represent numbers. The context of the candy shop helps students connect to the value of digits. The action of unpacking a box links directly to the action of decomposing 1 hundred and representing it as 10 tens. In addition, the concrete representation of candy aids in the transition to thinking about numbers more abstractly. Hence, it is important to provide time for students to work with the candy shop context and concrete items as a precursor to engaging with numbers in the abstract. Counting cubes, connecting cubes, or Unifix cubes are examples of concrete models that might be used to explore numbers in the candy shop context. For example, one connecting cube can be used to model an individual piece of candy (1); ten connecting cubes can be used to model a roll of candy (10), and ten connecting cube "rolls" can be used to model a box of candy (100). Figure 1.2 provides a visual of connecting cubes used in this way.

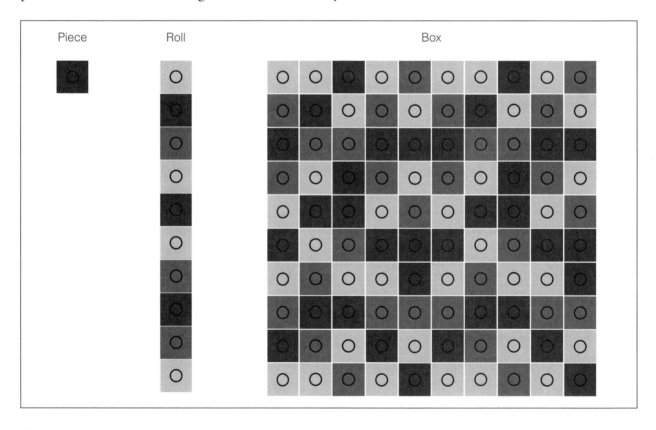

Figure 1.2: Example of a candy shop model.

Another effective model uses small beads strung on pipe cleaners. The beads can be viewed as individual candies and then as rolls when ten are placed on a small pipe cleaner. Ten pipe cleaners containing ten beads each can then be placed in a small box to represent 1 hundred in a candy box. Small gift card boxes work well for this purpose (see figure 1.3).

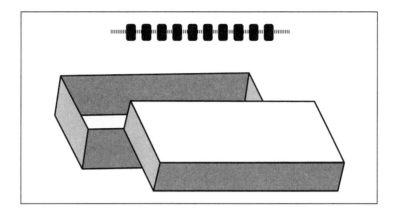

Figure 1.3: Beads on pipe cleaner candy shop model.

It is helpful for students to have many opportunities to use whatever tangible representation for the candy shop pieces, rolls, and boxes that you are comfortable implementing. This concrete representation allows them to build a foundation for understanding the ten-to-one relationship of place value. Once students are efficient with the concrete representation, have them use drawings along with the actual concrete model. However, students may or may not make drawings depicting the actual concrete models that are used for the experience—they could draw pieces of candy instead, for instance. What is important is that students' drawings indicate the correct understanding about the place value process in the candy shop task.

Eventually, students will use numeric recording. It is important to not rush the process; some students need extra time with concrete models and drawings. Ultimately, students need to be able to connect their understanding of the concrete model and drawings to their ability to do the same tasks with numbers and their understanding of place value exclusively. This is most likely to occur if students are supported to move from a concrete model (objects representing the candy packages) to a representational model (basic drawings of the packages) to abstract representations (numerals).

While working through the task in figure 1.1 (page 13), students initially use connecting cubes to model and represent 347 as 3 boxes, 4 rolls, and 7 individual pieces. Next, they use the cubes to model different ways, such as 2 boxes, 14 rolls, and 7 pieces. From there, they transition to using drawings on paper. With scaffolding to help the students identify the single pieces of candies as ones, the rolls as tens, and the boxes as hundreds, students work toward identifying 347 as 3 hundreds, 4 tens, and 7 ones. They relate their experiences working with the candy shop structure to apply an understanding of the value of digits and ways to compose and decompose different numbers.

Using the candy shop structure is beneficial for students. Their experiences packing and unpacking the candy into boxes and rolls sets the stage for composing and decomposing multidigit numbers when adding and subtracting with regrouping. Particular strategies for applying candy shop strategies with addition and subtraction will be discussed in chapter 4 (page 71).

The Progression

An understanding of number concepts is fundamental in preparing students to work in the base ten number system. This understanding also provides the building blocks for students to engage in operations and algebraic reasoning. The progression of learning begins with students knowing number names, understanding counting, and knowing small quantities without having to count, such as recognizing that there are five objects in a set from sight. Experience working with groups of items leads to the ability to subitize, which will be described in more detail on page 18. Students begin reciting the number names, followed by counting from one then move to counting on from a given number. Next, students move from counting to subitizing. This is an indication of more advanced strategies because they learn to recognize the quantity of a group of objects rather than needing to rely on recounting the quantity. The progression of learning place value concepts begins with recognizing staged quantities, which leads to recognizing quantities as a compilation of parts. In recognizing that, students can use the important make-a-ten strategy. Eventually, students work to understand place value in three-digit numbers in grade 2.

Following is an overview of the progression of number concepts in kindergarten through grade 2. You'll note that counting and cardinality (number concepts) are addressed in advance of place value and operation concepts. It is important for students to develop deep and meaningful connections to the mathematical content at each grade level.

Here is a progression for counting and cardinality.

- Know number names and the counting sequence.
- Apply one-to-one correspondence when counting objects.
- Identify a small number of objects without counting (subitize).
- Count to 100 by ones and tens.
- Count on from a given number.
- Write numerals for sets.
- Count to 120 starting with any number.
- Count within 1,000 including skip counting by fives, tens, and hundreds.

Here is a progression that builds understanding of place value.

- Compose and decompose numbers.
- Make sense of representations of tens and ones.
- Compare numbers based on the meanings of the tens and ones.
- Make sense of representations of hundreds, tens, and ones.
- Compare numbers based on the meanings of the hundreds, tens, and ones.

Here, we'll detail the progression at each grade level.

Kindergarten

Prior to kindergarten, children likely have experience with number and counting. They might count their toys or guess to describe a quantity of toys. When young children guess how many objects are in a group, they are engaged in early development of estimation. They might encounter representations of numbers when using dominoes or number cubes. Sometimes, young children are able to identify a number of objects (like three pips on a number cube) without counting. In kindergarten, attention to counting becomes more formal. Students learn to count to 100 by ones and tens. When given a known set of objects, they are able to count forward from that number without needing to start at one. They begin to read and write numerals and use them to represent a set of objects. Students can understand the relationship of numbers to a group of objects when working with numerals 0–20. We will describe the development of these skills in greater detail in The Mathematics section of this chapter.

Students at this grade level compare groups of objects and determine if one group is less than, greater than, or equal to another group. Note that kindergarteners may begin this group comparison with alternative language, such as "smaller than," "bigger than," and "the same as." They compare small numbers, 1–10, when they are presented as numerals. They rely on strategies such as matching objects one to one to make comparisons when working with larger numbers.

Grade 1

In grade 1, students continue their work with counting and extend the counting sequence to 120. They also read and write these numerals. They are able to provide a numeral to represent a group of objects.

Students in grade 1 compare two-digit numbers based on an understanding of the value of tens and ones. They begin to use symbolic representations to indicate comparisons between numbers. Their work with place value is crucial for helping them view the digits of numbers as representative of the amount of tens and ones. They build on the work they did in kindergarten with numbers 0–20 and now apply an understanding of the representation of tens and ones that make up these numbers.

Grade 2

In grade 2, students build on earlier experiences and count within 1,000. They skip count by twos, fives, tens, or hundreds. They read and write numerals to 1,000 and connect the numerical representation to their base ten understanding.

Grade 2 students compare three-digit numbers based on their understanding of hundreds, tens, and ones. They continue using symbols to record the comparisons. They become more flexible with representing hundreds, tens, and ones and recognize that they can represent a number in different ways. For example, 10 tens can also be called 1 hundred.

The Mathematics

There are many concepts to consider as students build an understanding of number. The work they do in grades K–2 is critical in setting the strong foundation necessary to build on in future years. Students will need to become familiar with such ideas as counting, subitizing, number sense, and place value. Tools such as number cubes, dot plates, and the hundred chart are useful in supporting the development of these concepts. Students benefit from experiences where they are actively involved in sense making around number.

Developing Counting and Cardinality

In order to be effective with counting and cardinality, K–2 students need to be able to successfully meet four goals. First, they must know and be able to express the number names, and second, they must know and be able to express the number names in sequence. Students enter school with very different experiences, and all students need many experiences hearing items being counted. A nice practice activity is to have students count steps as they walk from one side of the room to the other, to the playground, or to the cafeteria. Students can also count papers that are being distributed to the class or count the number of students who will be eating school lunch. The more opportunities students have to hear the counting sequence, the more likely they are to internalize the number names and the order in which they must be used when counting.

The third goal is for students to recognize one-to-one correspondence. This becomes evident when students point to or touch items as they count them. Students may start with items in a line and then move on to groups of items that are not organized; this approach helps them understand that the order in which objects are counted is primarily irrelevant. Information about students' thinking can be obtained by the way students engage with a counting exercise. For instance, more sophisticated strategies involve sliding each object to the side as it is counted or mentally keeping track of the starting point and which objects have already been counted.

The fourth goal with counting is that the last number students say when counting a set is the total amount in the set—that is, the cardinality of the set. Students having difficulties may re-count the set when asked how many items are in front of them, even though they have already counted the items. Encourage students to count aloud when possible. This action will help you identify counting errors and will provide information that can be useful in supporting students to build on what they know.

Students will advance from counting single objects to grouping objects. Another term for this is *unitizing*. When students unitize, they view a set of items as a new unit. A connection of counting out ten individual objects and then renaming those ten objects as representing 1 ten is evidence of unitizing. The ten becomes a unit. This is a critical building block for place value and marks a transition from expectations in kindergarten and grade 1. In kindergarten, students think of the number 13 as 10 ones and 3 more ones. In grade 1, as students begin to unitize, they think of the same number as 1 ten and 3 ones.

Understanding Subitizing

The ability to look at a set of objects and automatically know the number it represents without counting is known as *subitizing*. Consider the example of pips on a number cube. The typical orientation of the pips is provided in figure 1.4.

Figure 1.4: Number cube.

How many pips do you see for the number rolled? You probably recognized how many pips there were without having to count them: you were able to subitize. This important skill leads to efficient strategies and fluency with arithmetic. Within subitizing, there is perceptual subitizing and conceptual subitizing. The difference between perceptual and conceptual subitizing is that conceptual subitizing uses an additional step. Once a quantity is recognized automatically, another action is applied. For example, it would be considered perceptual subitizing if you saw a number cube with five pips on it and recognized that as five. It would be considered conceptual subitizing if you saw that same orientation of pips along with another number cube with three pips, you would combine the three with the five to determine that there are eight pips without having to count each individual pip or to count on from one number cube to combine the pips on the other cube. Students build on their ability to use perceptual subitizing when they move on to conceptual subitizing.

Dot plates are another useful tool for supporting student thinking with respect to subitizing (see figure 1.5). One option for constructing this tool is to use circular stickers to create different quantities on paper plates. Each of the numbers, 1 through 10, can be represented in a variety of different ways. Each number model should be made on its own plate. The example in figure 1.5 illustrates several different plates with four dots.

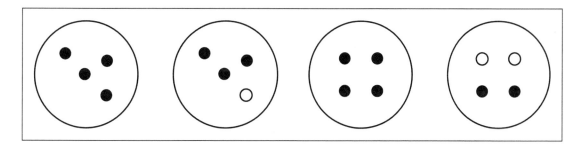

Figure 1.5: Example dot plates for the number 4.

The orientation or color combination of the dots on the plate will cause students to think about the numbers in different ways. Consider the representations for the number 4 in figure 1.5; notice that the first orientation may cause students to look at the dots as one less than five (conceptual subitizing), the second plate may cause students to see three and one more (conceptual subitizing), the third plate may cause students to see the quantity of four (perceptual subitizing), and the last plate may cause students to see the dots as two and two (conceptual subitizing). Different orientations and color combinations help students view the numbers in different ways. Students can even participate in making the dot plates and collaborate to come up with different representations for each number.

You can use dot plates in a variety of ways. You can flash a plate at the students and have them say how many dots they saw. This is something students can manage well in pairs. Students can also order the plates, match by value, or recreate what is on the plate using two-color counters. Two-color counters are counters that are shaded a different color on each side, typically red and yellow. Students can use the two sides to represent the different shades of dots. Another option is to create additional plates or cards to contain the number word or the numeral and have students match the dot plates with the other plates or cards. Moreover, students can compare quantities between two plates.

Fostering Number Sense

Students need time to build their understanding of numbers. You can support their efforts by providing appropriate structures. For example, students need to make meaningful connections to how numbers relate to other numbers. Anchoring to the number 5 is helpful for kindergarten students. The use of a five frame can provide a tangible representation. Two-color counters work well for students to create different ways to fill their five frame (see figure 1.6). They can learn to count on from a full five frame. They can also use the five frame to compare amounts with a friend who has a different number of counters on his or her frame.

Figure 1.6: Five frame.

Anchoring to 10 is also an important task for students. Ten frames can be used in a variety of ways. For example, students can combine two-color counters to make ten using two different colors. Using the two-color counters, students can explore different combinations of red and yellow to fill the frame, such as eight red counters and two yellow counters. They can flip the colored counters to adapt the combination. If they flip one of the eight red counters to yellow, they can represent ten as seven red counters and three yellow counters. Students can use ten frames in the same way that the dot plates are used: some may view a ten frame that is missing one counter as one less than 10, while others may view the amount through conceptual subitizing, by seeing it as a 5 and 4. It is helpful for students to share the ways in which they view the quantities as that clarifies their thinking to others and perhaps broadens their own views. Look at figure 1.7, and think of at least three different ways to describe what you see.

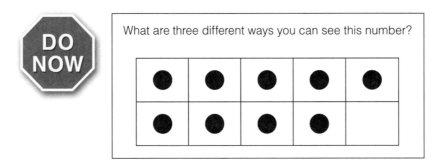

Figure 1.7: Ten frame.

Perhaps you used perceptual subitizing and automatically saw the number 9. It is likely that you were able to view the ten frame in these additional ways: one less than 10, 5 and 4, and maybe even 8 and 1. The important thing to remember is that students will benefit from activities such as these as they learn to make sense of numbers and to think of them in flexible ways.

You can use double ten frames for helping students make sense of the numbers 11–19. For instance, students could practice matching frames that represent a full 10 and additional counters to model each of these numbers. They can also match written numerals and number names to the frames. Double ten frames can also be used to help students anchor to 10. For example, using two ten frames, students can show nine counters on one frame and three counters on another. Students might have various ways to determine the total, but they are likely to see that they can slide one counter from the three counters to complete the first ten frame (see figure 1.8).

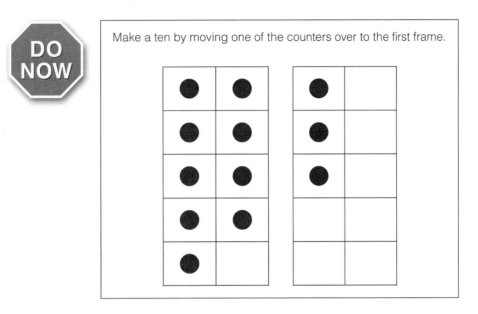

Figure 1.8: Double ten frames.

In this way, they are using the make-a-ten strategy in a very practical way. After all, it is more meaningful for students to make connections through practical application than it is to merely be told to use a given strategy. It is also important for students to have the opportunity to make sense of the frames using both horizontal and vertical orientations.

Using the Hundred Chart

The use of a hundred chart supports the transition from counting by ones to unitizing with tens. There are many ways to use a hundred chart. Models of two different hundred charts are provided in figure 1.9 (page 22).

The hundred chart can be used for counting, skip counting, counting on, comparing numbers, and so on. Students are likely to recognize the order of numbers on the chart, but they often struggle when they get to the end of a row. It is challenging for them to know where to continue as they point to numbers.

Ask students to discuss what they notice about the patterns on the hundred chart. Consider the layers of facilitation (I facilitate the whole class, I facilitate small groups, I facilitate individuals) for working through this activity, particularly when engaging the whole class in the task through questioning the students about the hundred chart. Through facilitation, you can help students notice that moving vertically in any row from top to bottom will increase the number of tens. It is helpful to use different colors to point out different patterns on the hundred chart. This approach is especially meaningful for identifying odd or even number patterns by shading the cells with odd numbers one color and the cells with even numbers a different color.

Blank Hundred Chart

Completed Hundred Chart

1	2	3	4	5	6	7	8	9	10
11	12	13	14	15	16	17	18	19	20
21	22	23	24	25	26	27	28	29	30
31	32	33	34	35	36	37	38	39	40
41	42	43	44	45	46	47	48	49	50
51	52	53	54	55	56	57	58	59	60
61	62	63	64	65	66	67	68	69	70
71	72	73	74	75	76	77	78	79	80
81	82	83	84	85	86	87	88	89	90
91	92	93	94	95	96	97	98	99	100

Figure 1.9: Hundred charts.

Experience using the hundred chart often leads to efficient counting strategies. Students may start out needing to count individual spaces on the chart but then learn through experience that when adding 10 or 20, they can just move down a row or two on the chart. This is an example of Mathematical Practice 8, "Look for and express regularity in repeated reasoning." Students see that when they add 10, they end exactly one row below where they started every time. The hundred chart itself can be seen as a tool to engage students in Mathematical Practice 7, "Look for and make use of structure." When students are prompted to explore the hundred chart and notice that it is made up of rows of ten and that each row of ten has similarities and differences.

Strategies for operations using the hundred chart are addressed in chapter 3 (page 51).

Focusing on Place Value

Place value is perhaps one of the most fundamental concepts that young learners encounter. It is also a topic that causes frustration for teachers because it is difficult to understand why students struggle with a seemingly easy concept. It is helpful to understand the ways in which students think about numbers. One unique feature of the base ten number system is that every number can be represented using only ten digits: 0, 1, 2, 3, 4, 5, 6, 7, 8, and 9. This awareness can help students realize the importance of finding the value of digits in multidigit numbers. Students will benefit from deliberate focus, building a strong foundation of the ten-to-one relationship in the number system.

Students begin with an understanding of representing quantities with a number and work their way toward being able to manipulate the amount of hundreds, tens, and ones to represent the same number in various ways. With experience, they come to know that numbers can be represented in multiple ways and still maintain the same value. One way to facilitate student understanding of place value is through the use of manipulatives.

Base ten blocks are very useful for teaching and learning place value (see figure 1.10). Specifically, base ten blocks are commonly used to help students build their understanding of the ten-to-one relationship of place positions in numerals. However, it is important to recognize the strengths and limitations of base ten blocks.

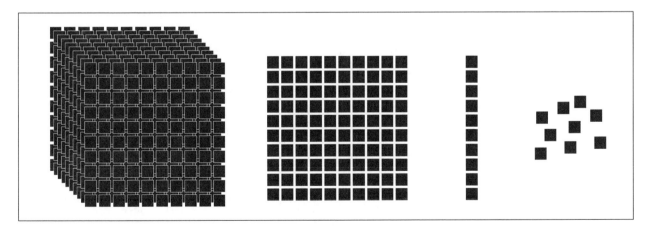

Figure 1.10: Base ten blocks.

These blocks are proportional and provide a concrete representation of numbers. What does it mean to be *proportional* in terms of representing place value? It means that the block representing 10 should be ten times the size of the block representing 1 and so on. What is an example of a place value representation that would not be considered proportional? Dollars, dimes, and pennies are often used to represent place value, and while money is something students often have experience with, it does not represent a proportional relationship between places. For example, the dime is not ten times the size of a penny.

While base ten blocks are proportional, their structure can still lead to misconceptions. Consider this: individual units (ones) are combined to create a ten. The tens are then combined to create a flat (hundred). Notice that the dimension changes from a length of ten units to an area of ten by ten. The dimension changes yet again when displaying the cube (thousand). This creates a model that is quite compact. The block that represents 1,000 does not look one thousand times as large as the block that represents 1.

Students can name the large cube in the base ten block set as a thousand but when asked how many hundreds there are in the thousand cube, they often say six. What is the basis for this error? The students see the six faces of the large cube as each representing 1 hundred and incorrectly deduce that the large cube is made up of 6 hundreds. They do not account for the units they cannot see. For this reason, as well as due to the compactness of the model, students' explorations of representations for place value should not be limited to base ten blocks.

The use of pennies may help students understand the ten-to-one relationship as they compare the length of one penny to the length of ten pennies. To prepare this model, use clear packing tape to secure the pennies. Lay the tape sticky side up and secure the ends; then line up 10 pennies side by side, leaving a small amount of space between each penny. Finally, lay another strip of clear packing tape over the collection of pennies, sticky side down, and trim the excess along the edges (see figure 1.11).

Figure 1.11: Taped penny model.

Repeat this process with 100 pennies to build a model of a ten as well as a hundred. Tape one penny on its own to use for comparison. Having these three penny strips is beneficial in helping students see that the 10-penny strip is ten times as long as the 1-penny strip and the 100-penny strip is ten times as long as the 10-penny strip. The 100-penny model provides a concrete visual that can serve as a point of reference when working with larger numbers. Hold up the 100-penny strip; it is approximately six feet long. Estimate the length of a 1,000-penny strip.

It would be inefficient to tape together 1,000 pennies, so instead, use string to make the length of 1,000 pennies. The 100-penny strip can serve as a guide to create the model. Was your estimate reasonable? Do you think your students would make a reasonable estimate of the length of 1,000 pennies? This is a great task to be completed outside or in a long hallway. Students can walk as far as they think the string will reach and then place their name on a strip of paper on the ground. They will likely be surprised at the length of the string and will gain a new appreciation for the number 1,000.

The Classroom

Now that you have explored your own thinking about place value concepts, turn your attention to what this looks like in the classroom. The included videos provide important insight into student thinking about place value. The first video demonstrates the foundational work that students need to accomplish in order to view numbers flexibly. In this video, students are asked to show the number 24. Watch the video in its entirety before proceeding.

   www.solution-tree.com/Representing_Two-Digit_Numbers

Now that you have had the opportunity to watch students actively engage in developing number sense, what are your thoughts? Consider how the instructional time is spent during the lesson. What do you notice about the amount of time spent exploring? Exploration involves students observing, wondering, questioning, and responding to each other and to the teacher. What tools does the teacher provide for the students? How does the teacher facilitate discussion?

Making sense of numbers requires dedicated time. It would be efficient for the teacher to tell and perhaps model the different ways to show 24, but what would be lost is the opportunity for students to make personal connections to the representations of numbers. It is sometimes difficult to view the teaching role as something more than just providing information. Notice that the teacher does not tell students how to model the number 24. Rather, she is more concerned with how the students engage with and use the blocks and drawings to express their understanding of the two-digit number.

Also note how students are not merely provided base ten blocks during the exploration. The expectation is set for students to model the number and also to represent the number with digits, number sentences, or pictures. It helps students to have concrete experiences before moving to representations and finally to abstract thinking about number. The use of the individual whiteboards and markers is effective in making the connection between a concrete representation and other forms of representations. Students' experiences with the blocks and whiteboards provide the support for them to engage in discussion about what they observe.

The teacher chooses to engage students in Mathematical Practice 3, "Construct viable arguments and critique the reasoning of others." It is important to note that the teacher carefully observes students working through the task. Her awareness provides the opportunity for her to highlight student work that leads to a meaningful discussion. She selects student work that allows the discussion to address the important concept of using different representations of the same number. Initially, she does this in a small group using layers of facilitation (I facilitate the whole class, I facilitate small groups, I facilitate individuals) to help individual students engage in the learning process by asking a student if her classmate is showing the same amount even though it looks different. Next, she shows drawings by two students who have modeled 24 in different ways. A third student shares that they both show 24, but they are not the same because of the use of different amounts of tens and ones. The experience of using tangible items to explore numbers helps students recognize that numbers can be shown in different ways. These important experiences and discussions establish a foundation for working with place value with larger numbers and ultimately for manipulating numbers in flexible ways in more complex problems.

In the next video, you will observe common struggles embedded inside a learning progression centered on the use of the candy shop structure to make sense of place value. Examine the struggles of students as they work through a natural progression of understanding and application of skills with place value concepts. A more in-depth description of the specific instructional decisions that move the thinking of students forward in a meaningful way follows.

Watch the video clip in its entirety before proceeding.

www.solution-tree.com/Introducing_Place
_Value_With_the_Candy_Shop

Now that you have had the opportunity to view a group of second-grade students using the candy shop model, what are your thoughts? What insights did you gain about student understanding? What part does student discussion play in providing these insights? In what ways do students use the connecting cubes? How are efficiency and accuracy addressed throughout the lesson?

It is important to note that as students manipulate the physical model of the cubes in the context of packaged candy, they make important connections to the structure of groups of items. Initially, the students are tasked with thinking about how the candy might be packaged. When a student states that he thinks there are 10 pieces of candy in a roll and 10 rolls in each box, this indicates that he has had experiences working with groupings of ten. This important foundation is further explored as the teacher asks students to determine how many pieces are in a box.

Students will follow a natural progression from counting by ones to counting by tens. In the video, many of the students count each individual piece of candy rather than automatically counting the group-ings of ten. It is important that students are provided the opportunity to explore this strategy, although it is not as efficient as counting by tens. You must allow students to have many different experiences so they can learn through experience that it is more efficient to count by tens. This is not a process that should be rushed.

One student in the video states that her classmate says there are 100, but her thought is that there are probably only 70 or 60 because there are not a lot of cubes. This is an indication that perhaps she was counting by ones and did not have time to complete the count. Her experience with 100 is not related to a concept of counting 10 tens.

Also notice a student who shares that there are 100 pieces in the box. When asked how she knows, she relates to there being rows of 10 in the box. When asked how many rows of 10, she states 100. This is similar to the error that students make when they say there are 100 tens in the number 100, rather than identifying that 10 tens make up 1 hundred. These errors stem from a lack of understanding and exposure to different representations of numbers. It is a critical skill for students to be able to describe numbers in flexible ways.

When the teacher asks the students to identify the number of candies at their table (1 box, 2 rolls, and 4 pieces), one student says that there are 100 candies and another student says there are 124 pieces. After discussing within their groups, a new response of 106 is shared. The student counts the box as 100 pieces, but then counts the 2 rolls and the 4 pieces in the same way as ones. It is often challenging for students to look at a grouping of ten and name it correctly. The transition from calling it 10 ones to calling it 1 ten may seem trivial, but students often struggle to make the connections of counting by units. In other words, the student in the video relates to the box being named a hundred but when looking at the remaining 2 tens and 4 ones, she begins to count by ones. This is an indication of her difficulty with unitizing tens. If she were asked how many rolls of ten she had, she likely could have stated two, but the link back to those two having the value of 20 would be a struggle.

Another important step for students to make is in regard to how they view the box of one hundred pieces of candy. They progress from counting one hundred individual pieces to counting by tens, but then they struggle to make the distinction of calling the box a hundred rather than continuing to count by tens.

The goal in using the candy shop structure is to provide students with a meaningful context to think flexibly about grouping in base ten. Next, take a closer look at instructional moves present in the video. Consider how your mathematics lessons engage students in making deep and meaningful connections to the content. Think about instructional choices that can increase student engagement and sense making during mathematics.

TQE Process

At this point, it may be helpful to watch the second video again. Pay close attention to the tasks, questioning, and opportunities to collect evidence of student learning.

The TQE process can help you frame your observations. Teachers who have a deep understanding of the mathematics they teach:

- Select appropriate *tasks* to support identified learning goals
- Facilitate productive *questioning* during instruction to engage students in the Mathematical Practices
- Collect and use student *evidence* in the formative assessment process during instruction

This lesson's *task* is designed to help students learn effective and efficient strategies for using groupings of ten to create 1 hundred through the context of a candy shop. Connecting the structure of groupings of ten to 1 hundred is done through the manipulation of physical objects, in this case snap cubes used to represent pieces of candy. The physical objects help students see, touch, count, and combine these objects in meaningful ways to make sense of the problem and of place value. The candy shop context also makes the idea of place value less abstract by thinking of tens and hundreds as packages. Once the students make sense of the features of the candy shop design, the teacher then asks them to determine how many "candies" are on each table. This sequencing in the task is an important feature, as the learning goal is to develop the understanding of groupings by tens—10 ones make 1 ten and 10 tens make 1 hundred—and then apply that knowledge to a contextual problem. The context of the candy shop models the structure of place value in base ten, and the teacher's instruction and facilitation engages students in Mathematical Practice 7, "Look for and make use of structure."

The teacher uses *questioning* in this lesson to ensure students understand the organization of the candies into groups of ten and how these groups are used to develop one group of 1 hundred. The teacher visits the first small group and asks, "What are you doing?" as a student is working to determine how many pieces are in one box. As noted previously, the student responds that her classmate says there are 100, but she thinks it is probably 70 or 60. The teacher turns to the classmate and asks her to make sense of there being 100 in the box. The classmate shares how she counted by 10 ten times and it equaled 100. Next, the teacher asks the student who thinks that there are 70 or 60 pieces in the box, "What does she mean by that?" Here she uses questioning to build a shared understanding among the students and to allow them to help others make sense of their thinking. The teacher is reinforcing her classroom norms of having students explain and justify their solutions, make sense of each other's solutions, and say when they don't understand or don't agree. These norms need to be established in the whole-class setting as well as in small groups.

Note that in the teacher's questioning style, it is often the students who are doing the thinking. When a student asks a question, the teacher often responds with another question, and sometimes the teacher's question is directed to another student. This allows the students to learn from each other, with the teacher guiding the instruction based on the learning goals of the task. The teacher knows the intended outcomes of the lesson and uses questions to guide students to those outcomes.

The teacher is also collecting *evidence* of student learning throughout the task. When she brings the class back together, one of the students shares that there are 100 pieces in the box. The teacher could be happy—mission accomplished, correct answer provided—and continue with the lesson. But the teacher knows that this is a key understanding in the lesson. She knows she needs to collect more evidence to be sure this student, and other students in the class, know how to determine that there are 100 pieces in the box. She intentionally asks, "How did you know?" This important question provides insight into student thinking and can bring misconceptions to the surface. A student says, "Because of its rows of ten in a box." Again, the teacher delves deeper with, "And how many rows of ten?" By asking this question, she is able to hear that the student believes there are 100 rows. At this point, the teacher could just correct the student but instead asks, "Are there 100 rows of ten in that box?" This provides the student the opportunity to reflect on her response and correct the mistake. It is important to know where the key points are in a task in order to know when to delve deeply into student thinking and reasoning. A key learning goal of this task is for students to see the structure of 10 ones make 1 ten and 10 tens make 1 hundred. The teacher purposefully collects more evidence on this goal to ensure students' understanding is deep.

An additional consideration is how to recognize and respond to student misconceptions. In the next section, you will review number sense and place value topics as they relate to common errors of students. This will provide another plan of action to consider as you address misconceptions by recognizing their source and thinking about ways to assist young learners.

The Response

Students are likely to make predictable errors as they learn to count and to identify the quantity of a set of objects. Initial errors include counting out of sequence, particularly when they first begin to count beyond 10. They have likely heard the number names but have not had enough exposure to the counting sequence to make sense of it.

Common errors include students counting a set more quickly than they point to the items and knowing the sequence of number names but not attributing what they are saying to the quantity they are attempting to count. This can lead to counting items more than once or missing items as they are counting. Students may also lose track of where they started counting and then struggle with knowing when to stop. In addition, students are likely to make errors when writing numbers. Before they develop a solid understanding of place value, they often confuse the placement of the digits in two-digit numbers. For example, they may write 81 when they are trying to write 18. With this particular number, the number name also contributes to the confusion, as "eight" is the first numeral heard in 18.

As students learn to count, note that they may use inefficient strategies. For instance, some students who have to count a set of 100 items recognize the efficiency of grouping small subsets of items and counting by two, five, or ten, while other students count the objects singularly. Another point where inefficiency arises in early counting is when students lose track of the counting process due to some distraction, stop the process, and cannot start counting again with the number they were at when they stopped the counting process; instead, the student has to start the counting process over.

So, how do you identify these errors, and how do you respond to them? Finding time to meet one on one with each of your students to determine their errors helps, but you may not be able to do this on a regular basis for all students. One way to identify students' strategies is to keep a clipboard with their names written on index cards. Make it a goal to write notes about the counting processes of at least four or five students each day. Determine their counting skills and errors while they engage in meaningful tasks such as counting and grouping items and recording how many.

Once you have collected specific information on individual students, you begin to address their challenges. Young learners need concrete exposure to counting tasks. It is important for students to be successful in providing a correct counting sequence, but students also must understand what it means when they communicate a number. It may be helpful for students to keep a written number line at their learning space. On the line, provide the numerical and written representation for numbers. Students can use connecting cubes that have been prepared in advance to model each number. For example, ten red snap cubes can be connected together and then additional snap cubes in yellow can be used to show a number more than 10. This helps students connect the idea that ten cubes and some more cubes can model numbers between 10 and 20. A blank hundred chart can also serve as a tool to support students' development of counting. Students can use the hundred chart to document their progress with counting.

They can also use the chart to practice counting on from a given number and counting back from a given number, two very important skills for counting that are prerequisites for addition and subtraction.

Be sure to anticipate the challenges students face when learning about place value. Students may be able to demonstrate surface-level understanding of the value of digits but lack the ability to apply a deep understanding of the relative values of digits. This lack of depth will have implications as students work on subsequent skills. The use of various manipulatives is important. Equally important is *how* the manipulatives are used. Students should be able to use them as representations and models of their thinking. When you allow students to choose their models, you are provided insight into their representations as they engage in Mathematical Practice 5, "Use appropriate tools strategically." Your use of manipulatives as demonstration materials or you telling students which manipulatives to use will not have the same impact on student learning.

In this chapter, you have examined several ways to help students build a deep understanding of number concepts and place value. Students will benefit from opportunities to view mathematics as something in which to engage. Your role in helping students who are struggling with these early mathematics concepts begins with identifying areas of concern. One of the best ways to determine student understanding is to allow students to explain their thinking. It is also helpful to engage students with one another. Kindergarten through grade 2 students are not too young to engage in Mathematical Practice 3, "Construct viable arguments and critique the reasoning of others." In fact, when they are struggling to understand number concepts and place value, they benefit from hearing multiple explanations. In addition, when you listen to their responses, you are provided with insight into the specifics of their understandings and their deficiencies. Armed with that knowledge, you can offer experiences that will guide them to work through their misconceptions.

Reflections

1. What do you feel are the key points in this chapter?

2. What challenges might you face when implementing the key ideas from this chapter? How will you overcome them?

3. What are the important features for developing an understanding of number concepts and place value, and how will you ensure your instruction embeds the support needed for these features?

4. Select a recent lesson you have taught or observed focused on number concepts or place value. Relate this lesson to the TQE process.

5. What changes will you make to your planning and instruction based on what you read and considered from this chapter?

CHAPTER 2

Word Problem Structures

Word problems are extremely important when an emphasis of instruction is on teaching for understanding. Students make sense of mathematics by exploring it in real-world contexts. This is especially true as young learners develop number sense with adding and subtracting. You must be intentional about providing students with word problems to solve and even having them write their own word problems.

The Challenge

Prior to reading further, write your own word problems according to the directions in figure 2.1. Once you write these word problems, set them aside. You will refer to them later after exploring word problems more deeply.

Write four word (or story) problems: one addition, one subtraction, one multiplication, and one division.

Figure 2.1: Word problem task.

In this chapter, you will make sense of word problem structures. The focus is primarily on addition and subtraction problems. However, since so much of what is addressed in the primary grades leads to readiness for multiplication and division, we will briefly address word problems supportive of these operations as well. Research demonstrates that kindergarten students can solve a variety of problem types, including multiplication and division, as long as the students can act out the action of the problem (Carpenter, Ansell, Franke, Fennema, & Weisbeck, 1993). To explore this concept, unpack the set of word problems provided in the word problem sorting task (see figure 2.2, page 32). We've adapted these problems from *Children's Mathematics: Cognitively Guided Instruction* (Carpenter, Fennema, Franke, Levi, & Empson, 2015), which provides an in-depth look at word problems and how they relate to Cognitively Guided Instruction (CGI). Rather than attempting to replicate their excellent work, we use it to support the continued development of your knowledge of the mathematics you teach with respect to problem structures. In order to fully appreciate the experience of unpacking these problems, copy the problems provided in figure 2.2, and cut them out along the dotted lines.

Copy and cut out the individual problems. Then sort them in any way that makes sense to you.

Alex has 7 red pencils and 8 blue pencils. How many pencils does she have?	Alex had 15 pencils. She gave some to Jessi. Now she has 7 pencils left. How many pencils did Alex give to Jessi?	Alex has 7 pencils. How many more pencils does she need to have 15 pencils altogether?	Alex has 15 pencils. She has 7 more pencils than Jessi. How many pencils does Jessi have?
Alex has 15 pencils. Jessi has 7 pencils. How many more pencils does Alex have than Jessi?	Alex had some pencils. She gave 7 pencils to Jessi. Now she has 8 pencils left. How many pencils did Alex have to start?	Alex has 15 pencils. Seven are red and the rest are blue. How many blue pencils does Alex have?	Alex had some pencils. Jessi gave her 7 more pencils. Now she has 15 pencils. How many pencils did Alex have to start?
Alex had 15 pencils. She gave 7 pencils to Jessi. How many pencils does Alex have left?	Jessi has 7 pencils. Alex has 8 more pencils than Jessi. How many pencils does Alex have?	Alex had 7 pencils. Jessi gave her 8 more pencils. How many pencils does Alex have altogether?	

Figure 2.2: Word problem sorting task.

*Visit **go.solution-tree.com/mathematics** for a free reproducible version of this figure.*

How did you sort them? Did you make a group that represented addition and another that represented subtraction? This is a very common approach. How did you determine the operation? Exploring choices for sorting problems provides a window into how you think about word problems. A common way to sort them is through the use of key words, such as *altogether, how many more,* and *left.* However, key words can be misleading and should not be stressed during instruction. Consider the two problems in figure 2.3. Notice how the use of key words leads to the proper operation. *Altogether* indicates addition in the first problem, and *how many more* indicates subtraction in the second problem.

1. Emma has 8 key chains. Calvin has 9 key chains. How many key chains do they have altogether?

2. Emma has 8 key chains. Riley has 15 key chains. How many more key chains does Riley have than Emma?

Figure 2.3: Key words in word problems.

Problems like these cause a false sense of security and might lead you to think that key words are always helpful. The result is the all-too-common poster on the classroom wall that has words for addition and words for subtraction and is often accompanied by chants like, "Altogether means add."

Then students encounter problems like this:

> Emma has 8 key chains. How many more key chains
> does she need to have 13 key chains altogether?

In this example, following key word instruction leads to an incorrect answer.

Students who are taught to rely on key words will get this problem wrong because they will see *altogether* as the last word in the problem, indicating they should add 8 and 13. However, students who have been taught through engagement in Mathematical Practice 2, "Reason abstractly and quantitatively," will likely be successful with this problem because they will respond to the questions, "What is the problem asking?," "What do I know?," and "What do I need to do to answer the question?"

These questions are aligned with the kind of student thinking that occurs when instruction is focused on reading comprehension. According to research, students do not typically apply their reading comprehension skills when they are solving mathematics word problems. Students often do not consider those strategies or replace them with key word strategies once they realize they are solving mathematics word problems (Clements, 2011). Be intentional about supporting students to use reading comprehension strategies to make sense of mathematics word problems.

One useful strategy is to have students act out the story in the word problem. This is easier to accomplish when the story involves action. *Action* does not necessarily refer to movement but rather that something happens to an initial quantity in the problem. Consider the following problems in figure 2.4. Both problems include movement, but only the first problem involves action.

1. There were 7 sharks swimming around. Eight more sharks join them. How many sharks are there now?

2. There are 7 sharks and 8 barracudas swimming around. How many fish are there altogether?

Figure 2.4: Action and nonaction word problems.

Acting out the first problem with countable objects would involve beginning with seven sharks and then adding eight sharks to the seven that were there at the start. With the second problem, the sharks and the barracudas are already there so there is nothing to do to act out the problem. This is an important distinction for students who are beginning to make sense of solving addition and subtraction word problems.

Now, revisit your sorted cards. Which of the cards represent action? Look at the cards carefully and re-sort the eleven word problems in figure 2.2 (page 32) so that there are two piles, one with action problems and one with nonaction problems.

It is likely that you have five action problems and six nonaction problems. This is actually not correct, but don't worry about that for now. Set the nonaction problems aside and further sort the action problems into two piles, those that represent joining situations and those that represent separating situations.

If you had five action problems to start, you probably have two joining problems and three separating problems. Of the two joining problems, which would be easier for students to solve? It is likely that you chose this problem.

> Alex had 7 pencils. Jessi gave her 8 more pencils.
> How many pencils does Alex have altogether?

Which would be the easiest separate problem? It is likely that you chose this problem.

> Alex had 15 pencils. She gave 7 pencils to Jessi.
> How many pencils does Alex have left?

In both of these problems, the result of the action is the unknown quantity. In the joining problem, a student might solve it by starting with counters to represent seven pencils to show what Alex had to start, then adding eight counters to represent the pencils Jessi gave Alex. The answer would be the result of this action and could be determined by counting all of the counters. These problem types are *result unknown* problems and are named join (result unknown) and separate (result unknown) respectively (Carpenter et al., 2015).

The unknown quantity is used to name the other action word problems as well. If you identified two action problems, the remaining action problem is likely a *start unknown* problem, named as such because the initial quantity, or the quantity at the start of the action, is what is unknown.

> Alex had some pencils. Jessi gave her 7 more pencils. Now she
> has 15 pencils. How many pencils did Alex have to start?

The corresponding separating problem also has the initial quantity unknown.

> Alex had some pencils. She gave 7 pencils to Jessi. Now she
> has 8 pencils left. How many pencils did Alex have to start?

In both of these problems, the action itself is known, as is the result of the action. What is unknown is the initial quantity, or the start of the problem. These problems are referred to as *start unknown* problems (Carpenter et al., 2015).

The last of the action problems, if you sorted five action problems, has the unknown in yet another location. The start is known, as is the result. What is unknown is the action that must occur to solve the problem. The action of the problem is referred to as the *change*. Therefore, the following problem is referred to as a *change unknown* problem (Carpenter et al., 2015).

> Alex had 15 pencils. She gave some to Jessi. Now she has 7 pencils left. How many pencils did Alex give to Jessi?

If you originally sorted five problems into the action pile, what seems to be missing from the problems? Did you identify a join (change unknown) problem? You likely placed it in the nonaction pile when you were sorting action and nonaction problems. Look for it now. You probably missed it earlier because the action is actually implied in the problem. The action is described by the pencils Alex needs to get to have fifteen pencils altogether.

> Alex has 7 pencils. How many more pencils does she need to have 15 pencils altogether?

So there are six action problems and five nonaction problems.

The nonaction problems consist of problems that represent comparison situations and those that do not. The noncomparison problems are very similar to the action problems in that there are two distinct sets of quantities known. They are different in that the quantities are "already there" so no action is described or implied in the problem; there are two parts and a whole, and both parts are there from the start whether known or unknown. These can be referred to as *part-part-whole* problems (Carpenter et al., 2015). With these problems, either the whole is unknown or a part is unknown (see figure 2.5).

Part-Part-Whole (Whole Unknown)

Alex has 7 red pencils and 8 blue pencils. How many pencils does she have?

Part-Part-Whole (Part Unknown)

Alex has 15 pencils. Seven are red and the rest are blue. How many blue pencils does Alex have?

Figure 2.5: Part-part-whole word problems.

The last three problems from the nonaction group are the *compare* problems. These problems are different from the others in that sets are not joined together or separated but rather, as the name implies, compared. There are three different potential unknown quantities: the difference, the greater quantity, and the lesser quantity. Match each problem to its label before reading on.

Figure 2.6 (page 36) provides the three compare problems labeled by their unknowns. However, in each case, the question begins with, "How many more pencils does . . ." The question *could* have been worded, "How many fewer pencils does . . ." Thus, both of those versions are included for each problem type. Notice the similarities and differences between problem types.

	Difference Unknown	Greater Unknown	Lesser Unknown
"How many more?"	Alex has 15 pencils. Jessi has 7 pencils. How many more pencils does Alex have than Jessi?	Jessi has 7 pencils. Alex has 8 more pencils than Jessi. How many pencils does Alex have?	Alex has 15 pencils. She has 7 more pencils than Jessi. How many pencils does Jessi have?
"How many fewer?"	Alex has 15 pencils. Jessi has 7 pencils. How many fewer pencils does Jessi have than Alex?	Jessi has 7 pencils. She has 8 fewer pencils than Alex. How many pencils does Alex have?	Alex has 15 pencils. Jessi has 7 fewer pencils than Alex. How many pencils does Jessi have?

Figure 2.6: Compare problems.

Both problem types ("How many more?" and "How many fewer?") determine the same unknown quantity; however, students typically find one more direct than the other depending on the unknown quantity. The difficulty of problem types will be discussed further in The Progression section.

It is important to provide students with access to a wide variety of problem types. However, it is typical for teachers to use the easiest problem types during instruction. Those are the join (result unknown) and separate (result unknown) problems. To help identify the problem types used during instruction, a completed set of problem types, including those covered in figure 2.6, is provided in figure 2.7.

Notice that the action problems, consisting of join and separate problem types, are in the upper section. The nonaction problems, consisting of part-part-whole and compare problem types, are in the lower section. Row labels describe the problem type, and column labels describe the unknown quantity.

Return to the addition and subtraction word problems you wrote as part of figure 2.1 (page 31). What problem types did you write? If you wrote join (result unknown) and separate (result unknown) word problems, you will need to be careful to provide students with other problem types during instruction, as these are the simplest problem types and provide a limited window into addition and subtraction in context.

The Progression

Prior to solving word problems, young learners must develop their ability to count. Students apply concepts related to counting and cardinality as described in chapter 1 to solve word problems. Once students have met this milestone, they are able to explore using all four operations with numbers in context. Following is an outline of a progression for how the operations are introduced.

- Make sense of contexts that support addition and subtraction where the result of adding or subtracting is unknown.

- Make sense of contexts that support addition and subtraction with unknowns in all positions.

- Solve two-step word problems involving addition and subtraction with unknowns in all positions.

- Make sense of addition situations involving adding equal groups to prepare for multiplication.

- Make sense of contexts that support multiplication and division.

		Result Unknown	Change Unknown	Start Unknown
Action	**Join**	Alex had 7 pencils. Jessi gave her 8 more pencils. How many pencils does Alex have altogether?	Alex has 7 pencils. How many more pencils does she need to have 15 pencils altogether?	Alex had some pencils. Jessi gave her 7 more pencils. Now she has 15 pencils. How many pencils did Alex have to start?
	Separate	Alex had 15 pencils. She gave 7 pencils to Jessi. How many pencils does Alex have left?	Alex had 15 pencils. She gave some to Jessi. Now she has 7 pencils left. How many pencils did Alex give to Jessi?	Alex had some pencils. She gave 7 pencils to Jessi. Now she has 8 pencils left. How many pencils did Alex have to start?

		Whole Unknown		Part Unknown	
	Part-Part-Whole	Alex has 7 red pencils and 8 blue pencils. How many pencils does she have?		Alex has 15 pencils. Seven are red and the rest are blue. How many blue pencils does Alex have?	

			Difference Unknown	Greater Unknown	Lesser Unknown
Nonaction	**Compare**	"How many more?"	Alex has 15 pencils. Jessi has 7 pencils. How many more pencils does Alex have than Jessi?	Jessi has 7 pencils. Alex has 8 more pencils than Jessi. How many pencils does Alex have?	Alex has 15 pencils. She has 7 more pencils than Jessi. How many pencils does Jessi have?
		"How many fewer?"	Alex has 15 pencils. Jessi has 7 pencils. How many fewer pencils does Jessi have than Alex?	Jessi has 7 pencils. She has 8 fewer pencils than Alex. How many pencils does Alex have?	Alex has 15 pencils. Jessi has 7 fewer pencils than Alex. How many pencils does Jessi have?

Figure 2.7: Addition and subtraction problem types.

Addition and subtraction problems can take many forms, as explored through the problems in figure 2.7. These types of problems are used through the primary grades with different numbers appropriate to the grade level and students. Students begin with word problems and act out the context of the problems with manipulatives, like counters. Eventually, students calculate with the numbers in the word problems without relying on the context or manipulatives. They use the context of the problem to check to see if their answer is reasonable. When students solve word problems in this way, they are engaging in Mathematical Practice 2, "Reason abstractly and quantitatively."

Here, we'll detail the progression at each grade level.

Kindergarten

In kindergarten, students solve result unknown problems and whole unknown problems. It is typical for students to act out the problems by directly modeling the action in the join and separate problems. For this reason, these problems should precede the part-part-whole problems where there is no action to follow.

When solving a join (result unknown) problem, kindergarten students often count out the initial quantity, count out the change quantity, and then recount all to determine the result. As students count, they think about what the quantity represents. They are thinking of the action of the problem. This problem-solving strategy is called *direct modeling* and is the first problem-solving strategy young learners typically use (Carpenter et al., 2015). This can be problematic when there is no action, as in the part-part-whole (whole unknown) problems.

Grade 1

There is a very big jump in exposure to problem types from kindergarten to grade 1. In grade 1, students solve *all* of the problem types. They move from using direct modeling strategies to using *counting strategies* and eventually to using *derived facts* (Carpenter et al., 2015). Counting strategies include counting on from the first number or counting on from the larger number if it is not given first in the problem. Students will learn to apply their knowledge of one fact to determine a different, related fact—a derived fact. For example, if a student knows that $6 + 6 = 12$, then the student can use that knowledge to find $6 + 7$ because the sum is one more than 12.

Grade 2

In grade 2, students continue to solve all of the problem types encountered in grade 1 but with greater numbers. Students also solve multistep problems. For example, a student might encounter a problem like the following.

> Alex has 36 pencils. Jessi has 44 pencils. How many more pencils do they need to have 100 pencils altogether?

This problem combines a join (result unknown) context with a join (change unknown) context.

Students in grade 2 begin to explore problems with equal groups in the form of arrays. Arrays are rectangular arrangements of objects or pictures where each row has the same number of objects or pictures. For example, stickers can be arranged in rows. If there are three rows with five stickers in each row, there are fifteen stickers altogether. These experiences prepare students to solve multiplication and division problems in context in grade 3.

Grade 3

It is helpful for you to understand the future expectations for your students so you can build their foundation. Grade 3 students begin to explore multiplication and division in context. They use their understanding of repeated addition to develop a concept of multiplication. Likewise, they draw on experiences with repeated subtraction to develop a concept of division. They learn that there are two types of division problems: sharing and measurement. (We'll address these division problems later in the chapter.)

The Mathematics

There are many nuances that are often overlooked in regard to word problems. Exposure to different types of problems is important. It is equally important to recognize how the structure of the problems elicits certain actions and thought processes for students. In kindergarten through grade 2, students will need to be able to model addition and subtraction word problems with equations, represent addition and subtraction word problems with bar models, and (extending into grade 3) unpack multiplication and division word problems. Awareness of the thought processes involved when solving word problems will help as you support your students in developing these skills.

Modeling Addition and Subtraction Word Problems With Equations

When students engage in Mathematical Practice 4, "Model with mathematics," they represent contexts mathematically; they *mathematize* situations. Situations can also be modeled with drawings, graphs, and tables, but for the purpose of this discussion, the focus is on equations. Figure 2.8 provides two word problems for you to model with equations.

Write an equation to represent each word problem.

1. Some children were playing in the park. Eight more children joined them. Now there are 12 children playing in the park. How many children were playing in the park to start?

2. The pet store sells dogs and cats. The store has 18 pets to sell but only 6 dogs. How many cats are for sale at the pet store?

Figure 2.8: Modeling word problems with equations task.

How would you solve the first problem in figure 2.8? Most adults would subtract 8 from 12 to get the answer of 4. This might have led you to write the equation $12 - 8 = \underline{\quad}$ to model this word problem. While this equation can be used to *solve* the word problem, it does not represent the *situation* provided in the word problem. *Situation equations* represent the action, or implied action, of the problem. *Solution equations* can be used to solve the problem. The equation $12 - 8 = \underline{\quad}$ is a solution equation but not a situation equation. The equation that represents the situation is $\underline{\quad} + 8 = 12$. This equation is both a situation equation *and* a solution equation, as situation equations can be used to find the solution as well. It is our position that the use of situation and solution equations provides a link between the structure of word problems, the equations used to model the problem, and the solution process.

What is the situation equation for the second problem in figure 2.8? Did you think it was $18 = 6 + \underline{\quad}$ or maybe $18 - 6 = \underline{\quad}$? Both are correct. The second problem is a part-part-whole problem and does not represent action or even implied action (even though dogs and cats move quite a bit, this is not what is meant by *action*). Because there is no action in the problem, the solution equations are also situation equations. For this reason, nonaction problems are ideal for beginning to explore fact families.

Return to the action problems in figure 2.7 (page 37), and write a situation equation for each of the six action word problems. Take note of the placement of the unknown quantity for each problem. Once you have completed this task, compare your situation equations to those provided in figure 2.9.

		Result Unknown	Change Unknown	Start Unknown
Action	**Join**	Alex had 7 pencils. Jessi gave her 8 more pencils. How many pencils does Alex have altogether? 7 + 8 = ____	Alex has 7 pencils. How many more pencils does she need to have 15 pencils altogether? 7 + ____ = 15	Alex had some pencils. Jessi gave her 7 more pencils. Now she has 15 pencils. How many pencils did Alex have to start? ____ + 7 = 15
	Separate	Alex had 15 pencils. She gave 7 pencils to Jessi. How many pencils does Alex have left? 15 – 7 = ____	Alex had 15 pencils. She gave some to Jessi. Now she has 7 pencils left. How many pencils did Alex give to Jessi? 15 – ____ = 7	Alex had some pencils. She gave 7 pencils to Jessi. Now she has 8 pencils left. How many pencils did Alex have to start? ____ – 7 = 8

Figure 2.9: Action problems with corresponding situation equations.

Notice that the unknown quantity naming the word problem (result unknown, change unknown, and start unknown) also describes the location of the unknown in the situation equation. Nonaction problems do not have specific situation equations, as discussed with the second problem in figure 2.8 (page 39). Write at least two equations that students could use to model each nonaction word problem in figure 2.7. Once you have completed this task, compare your equations to the samples provided in figure 2.10.

The equations for the compare word problems can be used for both the corresponding "How many more?" and "How many fewer?" problems because the situation does not change, just the perspective. Exposing students to nonaction problems provides the opportunity for you to see how students think about addition and subtraction in context. Are students more likely to add or subtract to solve? It also opens up opportunities for rich discussions regarding solution strategies.

Representing Addition and Subtraction Word Problems With Bar Models

Another way to represent word problems is through bar models (also known as tape diagrams). Bar models provide a visual representation of the problem. They help identify the role of the unknown. Consider the join (change unknown) problem from figure 2.9.

> Alex has 7 pencils. How many more pencils does she need to have 15 pencils altogether?

Figure 2.11 provides a bar model to represent the mathematics in the word problem.

		Whole Unknown		Part Unknown	
	Part-Part-Whole	Alex has 7 red pencils and 8 blue pencils. How many pencils does she have? 7 + 8 = ____ 8 + 7 = ____		Alex has 15 pencils. Seven are red and the rest are blue. How many blue pencils does Alex have? 15 = 7 + ____ 15 − 7 = ____	

			Difference Unknown	Greater Unknown	Lesser Unknown
Nonaction	Compare	"How many more?"	Alex has 15 pencils. Jessi has 7 pencils. How many more pencils does Alex have than Jessi? 15 − 7 = ____ 7 + ____ = 15	Jessi has 7 pencils. Alex has 8 more pencils than Jessi. How many pencils does Alex have? 7 + 8 = ____ ____ − 8 = 7	Alex has 15 pencils. She has 7 more pencils than Jessi. How many pencils does Jessi have? 15 − 7 = ____ ____ + 7 = 15
		"How many fewer?"	Alex has 15 pencils. Jessi has 7 pencils. How many fewer pencils does Jessi have than Alex? 15 − 7 = ____ 7 + ____ = 15	Jessi has 7 pencils. She has 8 fewer pencils than Alex. How many pencils does Alex have? 7 + 8 = ____ ____ − 8 = 7	Alex has 15 pencils. Jessi has 7 fewer pencils than Alex. How many pencils does Jessi have? 15 − 7 = ____ ____ + 7 = 15

Figure 2.10: Examples of situation equations for nonaction problems.

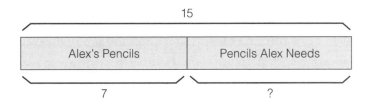

Figure 2.11: A bar model for a join (change unknown) word problem.

The bar model makes the known and unknown quantities in the problem clear. However, since they represent unknown quantities, they may not be proportional. For example, the bar in figure 2.11 appears to be broken into two equal pieces, but this does not necessarily mean that the quantities the pieces represent are equal. The result of the joining is known. It is 15. The start of the problem is given as 7, and the change in the initial quantity is what is unknown. The change is described as the pencils Alex needs. Thus, diagrams like the one in figure 2.11 can be used to provide a visual representation of the context of the problem, just not to the proper scale, as there are unknown values represented in the diagram. The diagram is dependent on the situation. Consider how the bar model for a compare problem differs from the join problem. Figure 2.12 (page 42) provides a bar model for one of the compare (lesser unknown) problems from figure 2.10.

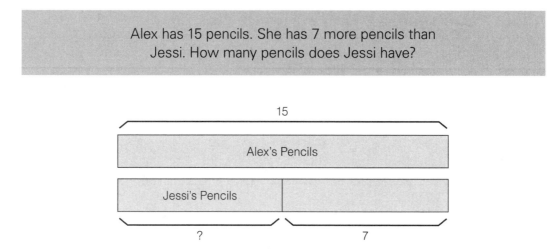

> Alex has 15 pencils. She has 7 more pencils than
> Jessi. How many pencils does Jessi have?

Figure 2.12: A bar model for a compare (lesser unknown) word problem.

Notice that in this problem, the 15 and the 7 refer to different sets that are not joined or separated. This is in contrast to the noncompare problems where there are two parts of one set. Compare problems build on students' earlier experiences comparing sets to determine if one set is greater than, less than, or equal to the other set (National Research Council, 2009). With compare problems, this idea is extended to describe the difference between the sets or to use the difference to determine the size of one of the sets.

Just as early experiences with comparing sets leads to solving compare problems for addition and subtraction, experiences with adding equal sets leads to work with multiplication. Formal work with multiplying and dividing is typically introduced in grade 3. However, it will be helpful for you to make sense of meanings for multiplication and division as you work with young learners to prepare for this later work.

Unpacking Multiplication and Division Word Problems

Just as young learners will create contexts for addition and subtraction problems, grade 3 students will create contexts for multiplication and division. With multiplication, both the number of groups and the number of objects in each group are known. What is sought is the total number of objects. A multiplication context for the equation $3 \times 4 =$ _____ could be:

> Paige has 3 friends. Each friend has 4 cookies. How
> many cookies do her friends have in all?

What is important to know with multiplication is that the first factor—in this case the 3—represents the number of groups, and the second factor—in this case the 4—represents the number of objects in each group. While the commutative property identifies that the product of 3×4 and the product of 4×3 are both 12, the situation equation warrants that the first factor designates the number of groups and the second factor represents the number of objects in each group; therefore, the cookie problem is modeled by $3 \times 4 = 12$ and not $4 \times 3 = 12$. This relates to work in the primary grades with repeated addition. Three rows of stickers with four stickers in each row is solved using repeated addition by finding $4 + 4 + 4$, because it represents three groups of four. The situation equation for the sticker problem is $3 \times 4 =$ _____ because the three rows represent the groups and the four stickers in each row represent the objects in each group. Return to the multiplication problem you wrote in response to figure 2.1 (page 31), and write a situation equation to represent it, being careful to use the form *number of groups × number of objects in each group*. While it is acceptable for students to write the equation with the factors in either order, teachers should be careful to represent the situation described in the problem.

What context could you use for the division problem $12 \div 3 =$ _____? Write a word problem for this division equation that begins, *"Paige has 12 cookies . . ."* What did you write? It is likely that you had Paige share her cookies equally among three friends or possibly two friends while Paige kept some cookies for herself. Creating these groups can be thought of as *fair shares* because the cookies were shared fairly among her friends so that there were the same number of cookies in each group. This situation represents what is called *sharing division*.

While some situations represent sharing, division can also represent measurement situations, which is referred to as *measurement division*. With sharing situations, the number of groups is known and the problem answers, "How many in each group?" With measurement situations the number of objects in each group is known and the question answers, "How many groups?" Measurement division might have nothing to do with actual measures like inches or cups but rather with measuring out quantities in groups of a given size. Rewrite the cookie problem so that it represents a measurement situation.

Figure 2.13 provides examples of sharing and measurement division contexts associated with $3 \times 4 = 12$.

---

1. Paige has 12 cookies. If she shares the cookies equally among 3 friends, how many cookies will each friend get? *(sharing division)*

2. Paige has 12 cookies. If she gives each friend 4 cookies, to how many friends will she be able to give cookies? *(measurement division)*

Figure 2.13: Problem contexts for sharing and measurement divisions.

The first problem in figure 2.13 answers "How many cookies in each group?" and the second problem answers "How many groups of cookies?" That is the distinction between sharing and measurement division. One finds the number in each group (sharing division) and the other finds the number of groups (measurement division). Return to the division problem you wrote in response to figure 2.1. Did you write a sharing or a measurement division problem? It is likely that you wrote a problem to support a sharing context. Just as with addition and subtraction for primary-grade students, teachers must intentionally expose intermediate-grade students to both division problem types.

While multiplication and division are not topics required of primary-grade students, students in primary grades are developing the prerequisite concepts and skills to multiply and divide. You need to be careful in discussing this topic with students so that the discussion will support further investigation in later grades.

The Classroom

Now that you have made sense of problem structures for the four operations, think about what instruction looks like when the focus is on sense making with word problems. The included video links provide opportunities to observe students in action. The first video offers a window into primary-grade students making sense of a word problem and solving it using direct modeling, counting strategies, and derived facts. The second video connects work in the primary grades to what is to come in the intermediate grades: grade 4 students write division word problems where the remainder to the division problem must be interpreted.

As you watch the first video, take note of the choice of problem structure along with who makes sense of the problem. As students solve the problem, keep track of the strategies they use. How are they similar? How are they different? Watch the first video before proceeding.

www.solution-tree.com/Solving_a_Word_Problem
_Where_the_Change_Is_Unknown

Now that you have watched the video, what do you notice? The objective of the lesson is reflected in the teacher and student moves. Who makes sense of the problem? Though the teacher presents the problem, the students also need ownership of the problem. Who shares the strategies? How are students supported to share their thinking?

The word problem in the video is:

> Stefan has 7 stickers. How many more stickers does he need to have 15 stickers altogether?

It is a join (change unknown) problem. The wording of the problem is such that students who are conditioned to use key words without making sense of the problem would likely add 7 and 15 to get an answer of 22. This occurs when the students see or hear the word *altogether* and assume they must add the numbers given in the problem because they have been taught that *altogether* means *add*. It is encouraging that this behavior is not evident in the video. The situation equation for this problem is 7 + _____ = 15.

The teacher gives students the opportunity to solve the problem on their own in ways that make sense to them. The first student who shares her thinking seems to have solved the problem correctly by looking at her manipulatives. She has 7 cubes in a row then a marker laid down to separate the 8 cubes in a row that follow the 7 for a total of 15 cubes. When she is asked how she solved the problem, she correctly says she "put 7 plus 8." When asked why she used 8, she indicates that she did so because the equation then equals 15. All seems to be going well. However, when prompted to say the answer, the student says 15. This is a common error when solving this sort of problem. Recall the situation equation. The 15 comes after the equal sign. This indicates, "The answer is . . ." to some students. This misconception is related to the use of the equal sign—it should be thought of as "is equivalent to." Notice that rather than correcting the student, the teacher redirects the student to return to the question, and the student is able to provide the correct answer of 8.

Following time for students to work out the problem independently, the teacher calls the class back together to share strategies. Consider where the strategies shared exist along the learning progression. Who used direct modeling? Counting strategies? Derived fact strategies? The first strategy shared with the entire class is based on a derived fact. Since the student knows the sum of 8 + 7, he can use it to *derive* the sum of 7 + 8. The second student who shares with the entire class seems to be on the verge of moving from direct modeling to a counting strategy. She uses all of the cubes to model the action of the problem; however, the language she uses to describe her process alludes to a strategy based on counting on from 7 to 15 to get an answer of 8.

Sometimes when students move from counting strategies to derived fact strategies, new errors arise. The student who adds 3 to 7 might have been beginning to use the make-a-ten strategy but makes an error in his thinking. Notice how the teacher begins with the student's thinking and helps him use the make-a-ten strategy to correct his error. Since this is such an important strategy, the teacher then has another student describe how he used the make-a-ten strategy to make sense of the problem.

The teacher concludes the task by recapping the many strategies used but then asks students how they might use a double to derive a fact for solving this problem. A student responds by describing how adding 7 + 7 can help find 7 + 8 through the use of the doubles-plus-one strategy. These strategies, along with the properties that support them, will be explored in more detail in chapter 3.

The second video is different than the first in that the students are not given a word problem to solve. The teacher gives them an expression and challenges them to write a word problem that connects to the expression and has an answer of 7. This is challenging because the expression is 26 ÷ 4. The quotient for this expression is 6 remainder 2, so a word problem that requires an answer of 7 is not immediately obvious. How does the teacher facilitate student engagement with this challenging problem? In what ways does she scaffold instruction? Watch the second video before proceeding.

www.solution-tree.com/Interpreting_the
_Remainder_in_Word_Problems

First, the teacher supports students to make sense of the problem. The students see that there is a remainder but also that they need to find a way to address that in the word problem so the answer to the word problem is 7. Initially, the students are not successful. They write a word problem that represents 26 ÷ 4, but the answer to the word problem they write is 6. At this point, it is typical for teachers to swoop in with their capes on to save the day as they rush to help the students; however, in the process, these teachers solve the problem. When this occurs, learning opportunities are lost for students. Why do so many teachers engage in this sort of behavior? It is likely due to their own discomfort at seeing their students struggle. Instead, in this video, the teacher helps students see the error and redirects them to their goal. She then gives students processing time to achieve success with the problem.

Notice that the first problem written is a sharing division problem. Ultimately, the students write a measurement division problem to meet the requirements of the task. Because the teacher does not use the gradual release of responsibility model by first writing a similar word problem for the students, the teacher is supporting student engagement in Mathematical Practice 1, "Make sense of problems and persevere in solving them." She is facilitating the whole class and small groups to do the sense making.

TQE Process

At this point, it may be helpful to watch the first video again (page 44). Pay close attention to the tasks, questioning, and opportunities to collect evidence of student learning.

The TQE process can help you frame your observations. Teachers who have a deep understanding of the mathematics they teach:

- Select appropriate *tasks* to support identified learning goals

- Facilitate productive *questioning* during instruction to engage students in the Mathematical Practices

- Collect and use student *evidence* in the formative assessment process during instruction

The *task* for this lesson is for students to make sense of a join (change unknown) word problem. The students are told to make sense of the problem in their own way; the teacher does not model how she expects the students to represent the problem. This freedom of choice supports Mathematical Practice 5, "Use appropriate tools strategically." The teacher then asks students to share their thinking in order to see which of the strategies she has anticipated the students will use. When she does not see one of the strategies she anticipates, she includes it by asking the class if there was a double that would help determine the answer. Here, the teacher focuses on Mathematical Practice 7, "Look for and make use of structure." She helps students see the connection to the use of the commutative property of addition when she has the student share how he switched the order of the addends and the associate property of addition when she asks students how they were able to apply the make-a-ten strategy and the doubles-plus-one strategy to determine the solution to the problem. Since one of the teacher's goals is to have students apply those properties, it is important that the addends in the problem she selected are near doubles and that one addend is close to ten. This is why the teacher chose 7 as the known addend and 15 as the sum. This task allows the teacher to have students demonstrate that there can be many different approaches to correctly determine the solution.

The teacher uses *questioning* in this lesson to allow students to correct their own errors rather than telling the students they are wrong and how they should fix their thinking. Using questioning to make these adjustments allows students to use their own reasoning to correct their errors, with the teacher guiding them to correctly make sense of the task. While it is important to question students when they make errors, it is also important to question students when they don't make errors to help them make sense of what they're doing. Consider the questions the teacher asks of the first student, who responds that the answer is 15. While the student's thinking is correct, the student selects the sum as the correct answer rather than the missing addend. The teacher addresses this common misconception and helps the student to the correct answer. She uses questioning to focus on the learning goals of students making sense of a join (change unknown) problem type and examining multiple student-generated strategies to solve it.

The teacher collects *evidence* regarding what students know and what they still need to learn. She learns that the student who indicates that the answer is 15 might need more word problems with change unknown and start unknown structures to be certain that the student does not assume that the answer is always the result of the action in join and separate word problems. She also learns which strategies students use when they have the choice, whether direct modeling, counting, or derived fact strategies. She sees that none of the students in the class used the key word strategy, so it is not mentioned in the lesson as it is a strategy the teacher hopes to avoid. Based on her observations, the teacher has evidence of which students will need additional experiences to help push them along the learning progression to more efficient ways of calculating based on the strategies they are currently using. Some students, especially those who are already using derived fact strategies, will need additional challenges so that they, too, have the opportunity to engage with problems they do not have an immediate answer for. The evidence collected provides the teacher with a guide to how well each student understands solving join (change unknown) problems using strategies.

The Response

The main area of difficulty students experience in solving word problems occurs when students do not have a firm grasp on counting and cardinality. If students do not know the numerical value represented by a number name (students can read *fifteen* but may not know how to represent fifteen objects), do not know the correct counting sequence, do not have one-to-one correspondence, and do not know that the last number counted names the set, they cannot solve word problems. Developing these skills must be an emphasis of prekindergarten and kindergarten instruction. Once students have mastered these prerequisite skills, difficulty in solving word problems often stems from students not being able to translate the words of the problem into a mathematical situation. In some cases, key word instruction is used as an attempt to address this issue. However, if you teach students to focus on key words, they tend to do so at the expense of reasoning and sense making. Key word instruction has no place in primary-grade mathematics and should be replaced by acting out the problem or determining responses to "What is the problem asking?," "What do I know?," and "What do I need to do to answer the question?"

Result unknown and whole unknown problems are simpler for students to solve. Start unknown problems are much more difficult for students. Keep track of the problem structures you use during instruction and which students experience success and which struggle with specific problems so you can provide extra support with those problem types. You can use a blank word problem chart similar to the one provided in figure 2.14 (page 48) to record this type of information.

			Result Unknown	Change Unknown	Start Unknown
Action	**Join**				
	Separate				
			Whole Unknown		**Part Unknown**
Nonaction	**Part-Part-Whole**				
			Difference Unknown	**Greater Unknown**	**Lesser Unknown**
	Compare	"How many more?"			
		"How many fewer?"			

Figure 2.14: Blank chart for addition and subtraction problem types.

*Visit **go.solution-tree.com/mathematics** for a free reproducible version of this figure.*

If students are in the direct modeling stage of problem solving, be sure to use action problems so students can more readily act out the problem. Encourage students to use more advanced techniques like counting strategies. You can also have other students using those more advanced strategies share their thinking during classroom instruction, supporting Mathematical Practice 3, "Construct viable arguments and critique the reasoning of others." Students are more likely to accept and try more advanced strategies if they see that their peers are using them successfully.

Reflections

1. What do you feel are the key points in this chapter?

2. What challenges might you face when implementing the key ideas from this chapter? How will you overcome them?

3. What are the important features for success with different word problem structures, and how will you ensure your instruction embeds the support needed for these features?

4. Select a recent lesson you have taught or observed that focused on word problems. Relate this lesson to the TQE process.

5. What changes will you make to your planning and instruction based on what you read and considered from this chapter?

CHAPTER 3

Addition and Subtraction Using Counting Strategies

This chapter connects your understanding of number concepts and word problem structures with the operations of addition and subtraction using counting strategies. In the following pages, you will consider how to develop understanding of the concepts of addition and subtraction. The addition and subtraction learning progression begins with learners using strategies to solve real-world problems. We then blend the use of these strategies with the learning of facts to develop a deep meaning for fluency.

The Challenge

Our initial task for you provides a context for the addition of two two-digit addends (see figure 3.1).

Jamila has a total of 28 playing cards in her set. Jocelyn has 37 playing cards in her set. If the girls combine their two sets, how many playing cards would be in the combined set?

Figure 3.1: Adding two two-digit addends task.

What strategies can be used to solve the problem in figure 3.1? Make a list of different ways to solve the problem, and provide a brief description for each strategy. What was the first strategy you considered? Did you begin by using the standard algorithm? Other strategies demonstrate how to make sense of the task in meaningful ways, including the modeling of place value. The use of concrete materials such as base ten blocks can aid in representing the place value connection (see figure 3.2).

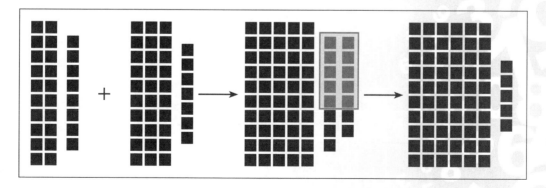

Figure 3.2: Concrete model of adding two two-digit addends.

The use of base ten blocks helps students make sense of exchanging 10 ones for 1 ten, showing how 28 + 37 becomes 2 tens and 3 tens to get 5 tens and 8 ones and 7 ones becomes 15 ones. Students exchange 10 ones for 1 ten so they have 6 tens and 5 ones, giving them 65 in all. This strategy is based on place value concepts, which will be discussed more in depth in chapter 4.

What about other possible strategies? Think about the student solution to 57 + 38 from figure I.1 (page 3). Recall how the student began with 50 + 30, then added 7 + 3 in the next step, and ended with adding 5 for a sum of 95. How might that strategy apply to the number of playing cards in the combined set? Were you able to solve the problem in flexible ways using counting strategies in a similar manner to that solution, or did you feel limited by your first consideration for a solution? This second solution relied on counting strategies rather than grouping strategies (in this instance, place value) because the student added 7 + 3 to get 10 ones rather than 1 ten.

You may have considered how context helps you make sense of the playing cards problem, and how you could have solved it if you encountered it as part of an everyday task. A flexible view of number might lead to using invented strategies such as one of the following.

- You can represent 28 + 37 as 28 + (2 + 35), which can be viewed as (28 + 2) + 35, or 30 + 35, which is 65.

- You can represent 28 as 20 + 8 and 37 as 30 + 7, and combining tens and ones gives 20 + 30 and 8 + 7, which could give 50 as the first sum, and 8 + 2 + 5 (splitting the 7 into 2 + 5) to give you 15 as the second sum and the combination of 50 + 15 = 65.

Where did estimation fit into your thinking? Perhaps you started by thinking about an estimate and then considering the reasonableness of your answer. The sum should be a little less than 70, as you are adding a number that is less than 30 and a number that is less than 40. Using estimation, either at the beginning of the problem-solving process or to check your answer at the end, is an important aspect of sense making in mathematics.

What about the standard algorithm? If you chose this strategy, you probably listed the numbers vertically, lining up the tens and the ones (see figure 3.3).

$$\begin{array}{r} {}^{1} \\ 28 \\ + \ 37 \\ \hline 65 \end{array}$$

Figure 3.3: Standard algorithm for adding two two-digit addends.

If you used this strategy, is the description of how you used it meaningful? Did you attend to precision with your language? This algorithm and the language to support it will be addressed in chapter 4.

The standard algorithm is not always the most efficient way to add two-digit numbers. People who are mathematically proficient consider other ways to determine the sum before simply moving to using the standard algorithm. For instance, tools such as the open number line can aid in making sense of other strategies. Base ten blocks are also helpful in making sense of multidigit addition. Moving to the standard algorithm too quickly encourages the viewing of multidigit addition as a set of unrelated steps rather than a flexible sense-making activity.

You may have felt that you completely understood the task when you determined the answer, but to be fluent, you should consider many different pathways and select the strategy that works best for a specific task and context. Being able to add multidigit numbers in a flexible manner is an example of Mathematical Practice 7, "Look for and make use of structure." When students are fluent, they can choose from many strategies, as well as consider which makes the most sense for the given problem. The goal with addition and subtraction in K–2 is to build understanding of the operation and use sense making along with appropriate strategies to build fluency. This view will support seeing the standard algorithm as just one strategy that may be used to determine the solution to a task.

The Progression

In looking at how the learning progression for addition and subtraction is developed, it is important to understand the links to the learning progression for number concepts and operations. These learning progressions are interconnected and built over time, both within an individual grade as well as across the K–2 grade band. Following is an outline of the important pieces that make up an addition and subtraction learning progression related to counting strategies.

- Compose and decompose numbers to 19.

- Solve addition and subtraction word problems within 10.

- Add and subtract within 5 fluently.

- Solve addition and subtraction word problems within 20.

- Apply relational thinking strategies to add and subtract.

- Make sense of and apply properties of operations as strategies to add and subtract.

- Add and subtract within 10 fluently.

- Add within 100.

- Solve addition and subtraction one- and two-step word problems within 100.

- Add and subtract within 20 using mental strategies.

- Add and subtract multidigit numbers using counting strategies based on properties of operations.

This progression of topics through the grades provides a structure for supporting students to build their thinking with number, addition, and subtraction. This conceptual understanding provides the basis for the processes embedded in the standard algorithms for multidigit addition and subtraction (described in chapter 4).

Here, we'll detail the progression at each grade level.

Kindergarten

Understanding the operations of addition and subtraction begins in kindergarten. Students gain experience working with numbers less than 20, decomposing and composing number values into tens and ones to build number sense and to solve problems. They use many different representations—such as objects, drawings, and their fingers—as well as actions to explain their reasoning. Many of these experiences involve word problems, based on specific problem types, as discussed in chapter 2. Students begin developing their fluency with addition and subtraction, and while they work with adding and subtracting within 10, the expectation is that by the end of kindergarten, they can fluently add and subtract within 5.

Grade 1

In grade 1, students add and subtract within 20 to solve word problems with unknowns in different positions, they also start to use a symbol to represent the unknown number in a problem. Objects, drawings, and equations are used to represent addition and subtraction word problems. These experiences are crucial to develop understanding of the relationship between addition and subtraction. Through situations and equations, understanding of the meaning of the equal sign is developed. As students make sense of the equal sign, they are able to use strategies based on relational thinking to make the process of adding and subtracting more accessible to them. Students extend this understanding as they apply the commutative and associative properties of addition as strategies to add and subtract. Although students are using these properties, they do not need to know the names of these properties. Grade 1 students develop fluency with addition and subtraction within 10 by using strategies such as counting on, making a ten, decomposing and composing, and using fact families.

Grade 2

In grade 2, students continue to develop understanding of the operations of addition and subtraction as they make sense of using many different strategies to solve problems. The focus throughout K–2 is on thinking and sense making, using conceptual understanding to motivate the rules and procedures students use to solve problems. The operations of addition and subtraction should be learned through strategies grounded in reasoning, strategies that reinforce self-invented algorithms, and ultimately, through applying standard algorithms.

The Mathematics

Students build on their understanding of counting to develop meaning for addition and subtraction. As students make sense of number concepts, with special meaning given to 5 and 10, they gain access to strategies based on composing and decomposing numbers for use in building addition and subtraction strategies. Fluency is developed as students learn to make sense of these operations both in and out of context. In K–2, students should come to understand early fact strategies, word problems and strategies for operations, operations using a hundred chart, operations using an open number line, and operations using partial sums. We'll provide opportunities for you to explore each of these topics in depth.

Developing Early Fact Strategies

Students use tools as they learn about adding and subtracting strategically. It is important to identify the ways in which students get to know numbers and learn to combine and separate them. Some tasks are better than others in helping students make sense of number combinations and support their understanding of adding and subtracting strategies. Often these tasks are focused on thinking about the different combinations to make 5 and 10. For instance, consider this problem:

Jasmine has 5 beads. Some of the beads are red and the rest are yellow. What are all the different ways she could have 5 beads?

Take a moment to think about this problem. Where does this problem fit within the word problem types described in chapter 2? Actually, it is not any of the problem types discussed in chapter 2, but it is related. It can be thought of as a part-part-whole problem where both parts are unknown. Consider how kindergarten students would make sense of this problem. What strategies could they use?

How did you organize your thinking in determining all of the different combinations of red and yellow beads? It is also helpful to consider how young learners might organize their thinking. If they were not sure about what to do, they could use beads or counters to help them make sense of the problem. What other tools could be provided to help them respond to this task? Figure 3.4 illustrates a five frame modeling five beads where four are dark and one is light. This five frame could be represented concretely with two-color counters so that four are showing the red side of the counter and one is showing the yellow side.

Figure 3.4: A five frame showing five as four and one.

Completing Jasmine's beads task requires students to decompose 5 in more than one way, which is an important task for helping students develop a flexible view of number combinations. The numbers 5 and 10 are privileged in the base ten number system. The importance of 10 is obvious, but 5 is also important because 2 fives make a ten. Students make sense of combinations to make 5 and 10 in many ways—by making drawings, using counters, counting on fingers, acting out situations, creating expressions—all aid in the development of strategies for the operations of addition and subtraction. Providing choice in the tools students use to make sense of these numbers is essential.

Allowing students to make sense of problems on their own is an important aspect of developing knowledge in mathematics. This represents Mathematical Practice 1, "Make sense of problems and persevere in solving them." Students need to take time to consider how they make sense of the problem first; then they need to consider how to solve the problems using self-determined strategies and tools that make sense to them. This represents Mathematical Practice 5, "Use appropriate tools strategically." In order for students to engage in this practice, they need to have access to different tools and the opportunity to make *their own* choices about which tools to use and how to use them.

It is important for students to have experience with tools that promote grouping by tens to represent numbers, to see how to decompose numbers, and to consider how to make sense of adding and subtracting. Ten frames are useful in these processes. Consider how numbers can be represented using ten frames, such as the representations of 14 provided in figure 3.5 (page 56).

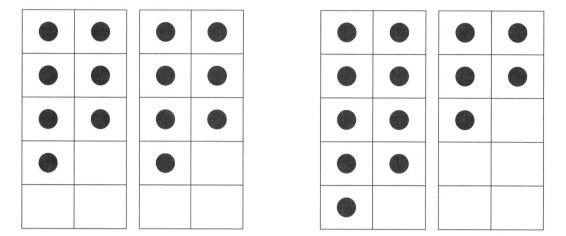

Figure 3.5: Ten frames showing fourteen in two different ways.

Describe the two representations of 14. How are they similar and how are they different? The first illustration shows 14 as two 7s. This leads to a strategy of composing a number using doubles, which serves as a strategy for quick recall of basic facts. Doubles also provide a foundation for repeated addition and lead to understanding the meaning for multiplication in grade 3.

The second illustration of two ten frames in figure 3.5 showing 9 + 5 leads to the all-important make-a-ten strategy. Students can mentally or physically move one counter from the second frame to the first to complete a ten frame, thus making a 10. This strategy is the most important strategy for students to explore in the process of developing fluency with basic facts and will be discussed later in this chapter. Application of this strategy in meaningful ways depends on relational thinking. Students must have an awareness that 7 + 7 is equal to 9 + 5, and that the same quantity can be arranged in different ways and still represent an equal amount. Many of the strategies students use to simplify the process of adding and subtracting when the answer is not known depend on relational thinking.

Reconsider the doubling strategy. How is it being extended in figure 3.6?

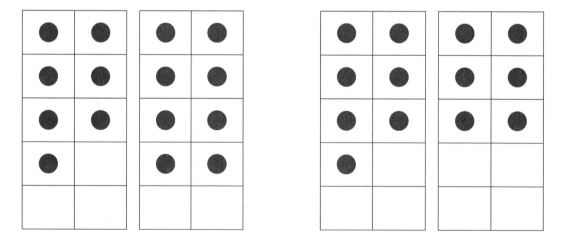

Figure 3.6: Extension of the doubling strategy using ten frames.

If students know the doubles fact, 7 + 7 = 14, how might they use it to find 7 + 8 or 7 + 6? These strategies are called doubles plus one and doubles minus one. They are accessible to students who already know their doubles facts. If students do not know their doubles facts, you can give them access to the strategy by simply providing the double, saying, "If you know that 7 plus 7 equals 14, how could you use that to find 7 plus 8?" Students' knowledge of doubles can be used to represent—and hopefully support the development of—a flexible understanding of numbers within 20. This flexible understanding supports making sense of addition and subtraction problems and leads to the development and reasoned use of efficient algorithms.

Think about how you solved the original task in this chapter (see figure 3.1, page 51). You may have represented the ones of 8 + 7 as 8 + (2 + 5), combined the 8 + 2 to get the sum of 10, and added the 5 to get 15. You can see how using ten frames, applying the make-a-ten strategy, and finding the sum of the two addends can work together to make sense of multidigit addition using strategies like these. It is important to consider the role of memorized facts and invented strategies in how mathematical understanding is developed. Reasoning strategies and fluency with addition and subtraction facts should be developed together, not one without the other. Knowing facts from memory is an important and helpful skill, but reasoning and having a toolkit of strategies to use in problem solving are just as important.

When students invent and apply strategies, they develop a deeper understanding of addition and subtraction. You may believe that knowing facts from memory is the most important element for young learners, and while knowing facts from memory is significant, it should not be rushed. Fluency is using efficient and accurate methods—both strategies and algorithms—to determine the result of a particular task (NCTM, 2000). As students invent and apply strategies, they are using and practicing with facts, which support the process of knowing facts by memory.

Making Sense of Operations Using Word Problems and Strategies

It is important that the connection between operations and word problems continues to be in place as you consider how understanding of addition and subtraction develops. Also, consider how the relationship between addition and subtraction can help make sense of problems, such as those in figure 3.7.

Write a situation equation for each word problem then solve each one in at least three different ways.

1. Gloria has 7 chocolate chip cookies. Javier gives her some more cookies. Now she has 13 cookies. How many cookies did Javier give to Gloria?

2. Brian has 6 apples. His dad has some as well. Together, they have 15 apples. How many apples does Brian's dad have?

Figure 3.7: Connecting word problems to strategies task.

For the first problem, how did you represent the situation? Did your equation represent the action of the problem? Your equation should support a join (change unknown) problem type, where the start is known (Gloria has seven cookies to start), the change of the problem is not known because you do not know the number of cookies Javier gives to Gloria, and the result of the transaction is known (Gloria ends up with thirteen cookies). This would be represented as 7 + _____ = 13, where the blank represents the unknown amount. Now, how would you solve it?

If you consider the situation, you know you need to add something to 7 to get a result of 13. If you know that 7 + 7 = 14, how could you use that to determine what to add to 7 for a sum of 13? This is a doubles-minus-one fact because, using 7 + 7 = 14, the student just needs to subtract 1 from 14 to get 13; instead of 7 + 7, the student knows to add 7 + 6. The missing quantity is 6.

With the make-a-ten strategy, the student would think, "I know that 7 + 3 = 10, and then I still need 3 more to get to 13. I know that 3 + 3 = 6, so Javier gives Gloria six cookies." The student is making a 10 by adding 3 to the 7. The student uses this to get to the unknown quantity by determining what still needs to be added to the 10 to get to the target number of 13.

There are other useful strategies for modeling this situation as well. A student using direct modeling could represent the problem with a drawing or set of objects to represent seven cookies to show what Gloria had to start. The next step would be to add cookies to show what Javier gives to Gloria until there are a total of thirteen cookies. As you add cookies, you would count, "Eight, nine, ten, eleven, twelve, thirteen." Then, recount the cookies added on to Gloria's original seven to determine that Javier gave her six cookies. This would represent a direction modeling strategy (see figure 3.8).

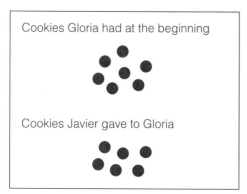

Figure 3.8: Using objects with a direct modeling strategy.

A student using the counting strategy, counting on, could use fingers, starting at 7, and then counting on until reaching 13, raising a finger with each count. The number of raised fingers the student would have when 13 was reached would indicate the number of cookies Javier gave to Gloria. Another model would be to use an open number line to follow the situation. An open number line does not focus on the equally spaced intervals of a typical number line but rather represents the thinking used to solve the specific problem. It is an excellent tool for reinforcing the make-a-ten strategy in a counting rather than grouping context. Begin with the number of cookies Gloria has to start (seven) then make a jump to the next 10. This requires a jump of 3. The last jump brings the total number of cookies to thirteen. This results in two jumps of 3 to represent the six cookies Javier gave to Gloria (see figure 3.9).

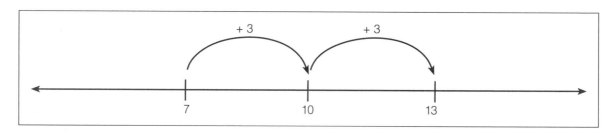

Figure 3.9: Open number line model for the cookie problem.

Any of these strategies can be used to correctly determine the answer. The strategy you choose should be based on how you make sense of the problem. When young learners decide which strategy works best for them, they are providing a window for you to see into their current knowledge of mathematics. These student-selected, and often student-created, strategies help you see how students make sense of the mathematics.

For the second problem in figure 3.7 (page 57), there is no action inherent in the problem, so there are several situation equations you could use to model the problem. You could think of it as addition or subtraction. This provides an excellent opportunity to link addition to subtraction so that students can make sense of the relationships between the operations. Students could solve this problem by thinking $6 + \_\_\_\_ = 15$ or $15 - 6 = \_\_\_\_$. Students could use direct modeling, counting strategies, or derived facts to solve this problem. Some students may count on using objects, drawings, or fingers in a similar manner as the first problem to find the missing value. The students engage in Mathematical Practice 2, "Reason abstractly and quantitatively," as they move from thinking that is supported by the context of the problem to thinking based on number strategies and back again. What is important is that students are able to use strategies that make sense to them and tools that support their reasoning. As students share their strategies with one another in the whole-class setting, they are encouraged to use more efficient strategies learned from their peers.

Showing Operations Using a Hundred Chart

A hundred chart can be used to extend understanding to adding and subtracting within 100. How does the organization of the hundred chart help you count by tens? Consider the task provided in figure 3.10.

Use the hundred chart to determine the value of 53 – 36.

1	2	3	4	5	6	7	8	9	10
11	12	13	14	15	16	17	18	19	20
21	22	23	24	25	26	27	28	29	30
31	32	33	34	35	36	37	38	39	40
41	42	43	44	45	46	47	48	49	50
51	52	53	54	55	56	57	58	59	60
61	62	63	64	65	66	67	68	69	70
71	72	73	74	75	76	77	78	79	80
81	82	83	84	85	86	87	88	89	90
91	92	93	94	95	96	97	98	99	100

Figure 3.10: Multidigit subtraction with the hundred chart task.

The hundred chart supports different ways of thinking about the problem compared to the standard algorithm. While the standard algorithm supports thinking based on grouping and place value, the hundred chart supports thinking based on counting. This could be counting by ones, tens, or other groups, but it is still counting rather than determining place value. One way to use the hundred chart to determine the value of 53 − 36 is to start at 53 and count backward 36 ones to get to 17. You could create a shorter path and subtract 10 at a time by moving up one row at a time on the chart, moving from 53 to 43 to 33 to 23. This would represent subtracting 30 from 53. Next, you would move single spaces to the left to represent subtracting one at a time, and you would do this six times, needing to move up a row after subtracting the first 2 ones. There are two areas that cause students to struggle with this subtraction process. The first is transitioning from counting where the ten is the unit to using one as the unit. This represents decomposing 36 into 3 tens and 6 ones. The second area of difficulty is when the student needs to wrap up to another row to count back by ones. This occurs when counting back from 23 to 17 by ones.

The ability to be flexible with units, such as when unitizing with ten as a unit and then using one as a unit, is important for students as they represent numbers flexibly. It is also a prerequisite for using place value to add and subtract with understanding. The hundred chart is a useful tool for focusing on unitizing with tens. It is especially helpful if the numbers are removed after students have made sense of the chart (see figure 1.9, page 22).

What if counters were placed on a blank hundred chart? Would you be able to determine the difference between the placement of the counters? Would you be able to use your understanding of unitizing to think about the relationship, even without the numbers on the chart? Consider the representation of counters on a blank hundred chart in figure 3.11.

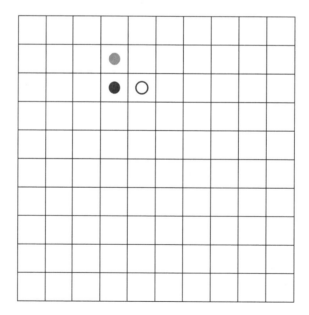

Figure 3.11: Blank hundred chart with three counters.

What is the difference between the black and white counters? Attend to the placement of the counters. Can you describe the relationship in more than one way? The black counter is one less than the white counter, and the white counter is one more than the black counter. What is the difference between the black and grey counters? The black counter is ten more than the grey counter, and the grey counter is ten less than the black counter. What is the relationship between the white and grey counters? The white counter is eleven more than the grey counter, and the grey counter is eleven less than the white counter. Did you notice how this discussion demonstrates the relationship between addition and subtraction? In removing the numbers from the chart, students are able to focus on the patterns with tens embedded in the hundred chart. This builds their understanding of the relationship between ones and tens. If you know the value of the white counter, what is the value of the grey counter in figure 3.12 in comparison?

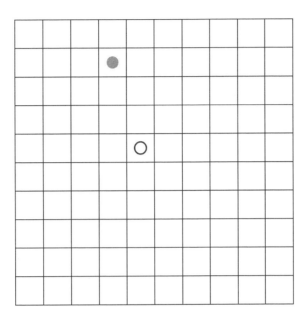

Figure 3.12: Blank hundred chart with two counters.

Is the difference 31 or 29? It is easy to see how both could be given as answers, but there is only one answer that is correct. Do not allow yourself to determine the corresponding number position of each counter but, instead, only look at the relationship between the locations of the counters to one another. This is an instance where the removal of numbers allows you to dig into Mathematical Practice 7, "Look for and make use of structure." Without numbers, the response needs to be based just on the relationship between the two locations on the chart, and too often, students make assumptions and determine answers quickly. The correct answer is 31. An incorrect answer of 29 is often determined by counting back three 10s and then subtracting 1 from 30 because of the last jump back. This represents an error in applying counting back to find the distance between two numbers. If you made this error, try determining the distance by starting with the grey counter and ending with the white counter.

Using a blank hundred chart allows students to build mental strategies associated with the relationship between unitizing and addition and subtraction. Thinking of addition as the inverse relationship to subtraction helps make sense of the problem. This inverse relationship is also accessible with the open number line.

Representing Operations Using an Open Number Line

The development of efficient strategies for adding and subtracting multidigit numbers builds on the strategies of single-digit addition and subtraction. Think back to the earlier discussion of 7 + _____ = 13 and the use of a number line model to represent the reasoning of determining the value of the unknown. Consider how to use an open number line to respond to the task in figure 3.13.

Subtract 53 – 36 using an open number line.

Figure 3.13: Multidigit subtraction with other tools task.

How did you use an open number line to help you make sense of this problem? How is the process for subtracting 36 from 53 represented on the open number line shown in figure 3.14? Examine the models in figure 3.14 to determine the strategy that most closely matches the process you used.

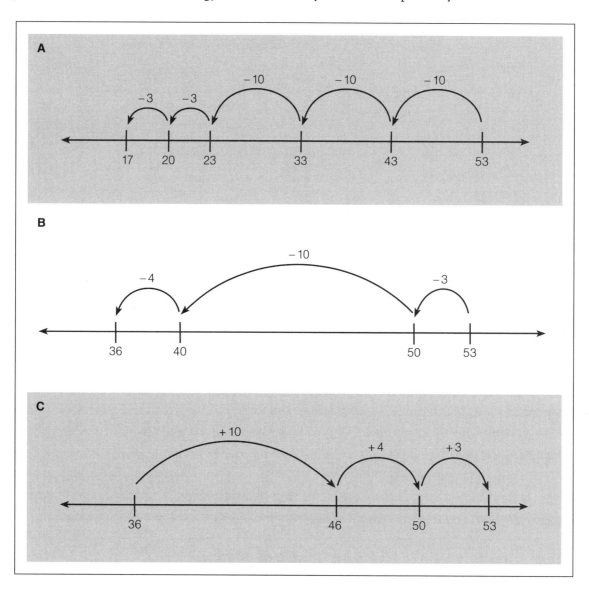

Figure 3.14: Strategies to show 53 – 36 using an open number line.

While the jumps that you made on your open number line might have been different, the structure you used should have matched one of the three strategies provided in figure 3.14. Strategy A represents take away, meaning 36 is being taken away from 53. The answer of 17 is located below the number line. In strategy B, the answer of 17 is determined by counting back from 53 to 36 and is represented by the distance signified by counting back. Even though 17 is subtracted to get from 53 to 36, the answer is 17 rather than negative 17. Your representation of counting back might look different if you placed the 53 to the left of the 36 on the number line. Since this is an open number line, that thinking would still be correct; however, it causes unnecessary confusion with students and should be avoided. Instead, the class should agree to place lesser numbers to the left of greater numbers when using the open number line. The counting-back strategy is similar to the strategy provided in strategy C; however, the jumps are made by adding 17 rather than subtracting 17, so this strategy represents counting up. When students represent solutions to problems on an open number line in ways that make sense to them and that connect to the task, they are engaging in Mathematical Practice 4, "Model with mathematics." They are mathematizing the situation of either take away, counting back, or counting up on an open number line.

Once students are comfortable adding and subtracting with two-digit numbers, three-digit numbers should be explored. Consider how to add 149 and 286 (see figure 3.15).

Add 149 + 286 using an open number line.

Figure 3.15: Adding three-digit addends task.

How would you think about this problem in a way that a number line strategy would work effectively? Consider one example of the number line model in figure 3.16.

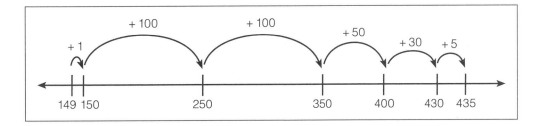

Figure 3.16: A number line model for 149 + 286.

Think about how you would explain all of the arrows and what they represent. Note that if you add up the individual jumps that the arrows represent, you will get the second addend of 286. In this model, the total builds, starting with the first addend of 149, to include the individual jumps needed to get to collective jumps totaling the second addend of 286. There are options in this approach, ones that allow for individual decisions and self-invented strategies. The choice to go from 149 to 150 by adding 1 first was just that, a choice—not a necessary move but rather a strategy. A different choice may have been to add 100 or 200 first, or to add 6 at the start. These choices create individuality that links to where you feel comfortable with the mathematics. Do you prefer to use fewer steps or to make numbers that are multiples of ten? As long as the total of the individual jumps adds up to 286, then you are using a viable strategy. As strategies are shared, students will learn different ways to compose the sum of two numbers. Efficiencies are developed through multiple experiences and learning the perspectives of others.

How would you use the open number line for multidigit subtraction? Consider the task in figure 3.17.

Subtract 436 – 82 using an open number line.

Figure 3.17: Multidigit subtraction task.

How did you model your strategy? If you discuss your strategy with your team, you may find that others use jumps different from yours. Did you think about what would be the most efficient way to subtract 82 from 436 mentally? Here is one possible model (see figure 3.18).

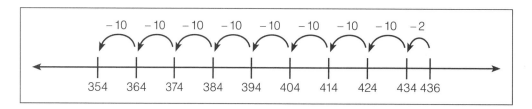

Figure 3.18: Number line model for 436 – 82.

How does this representation compare to yours? Just as in the earlier number line model for addition, there are many possible ways to model 436 – 82, and as long as the computations are done correctly, all of them can be appropriate models for how you see the subtraction. However, some will be more efficient than others. For example, counting by ones would not be ideal. You can also invent strategies without using tools, such as with partial sums.

Completing Operations Using Partial Sums

The partial sums strategy is often referred to as the *break-apart strategy*. It involves decomposing multidigit numbers by using expanded notation as a means to add "parts" of the sum in succession, which results in the overall sum of the task. Figure 3.19 displays the strategy.

Using the partial sums algorithm, you think of 149 as 100 + 40 + 9 and 286 as 200 + 80 + 6. You then add the following partial sums: 100 and 200 to get 300, 40 and 80 to get 120, and 9 and 6 to get 15. The actual sum is determined by thinking, 300 + 120 = 420 and 420 + 15 = 435. Notice how this method avoids regrouping but rather uses procedures more closely associated with counting strategies.

What is shown in the tasks and strategies in this section is how understanding of addition and subtraction evolves over time. This evolution is based on increased sophistication with the ability to use a greater range of

$$
\begin{array}{r}
149 \\
+\ 286 \\
\hline
300 \\
120 \\
+\ \ 15 \\
\hline
435 \\
\end{array}
$$

Figure 3.19: Partial sums model for 149 + 286.

strategies to make sense of addition and subtraction. Many of the strategies have elements in common, yet the differences allow the student to select more appropriate models for different problems. Procedural fluency involves students having access to different strategies and choosing the appropriate strategy based on the problem at hand. When students are successful with this, they are engaging in Mathematical Practice 5, "Use appropriate tools strategically." Students should not be required to master every strategy, but they should be able to make sense of the reasoning involved in many strategies to build their computation toolbox. Student-invented and student-selected strategies are critical to learning the operations of addition and subtraction with depth.

The Classroom

You have been working to make sense of the concepts of addition and subtraction. Now examine what addition and subtraction tasks look like in the classroom. The first video provides insight into a classroom where kindergarten students make sense of number pairs for ten. This classroom experience provides ideas for how to move beyond number pairs to set the stage for relationships between the numbers in the pair. In the second video, grade 1 students use multiple strategies to demonstrate how to determine the sum of 7 and 8. Both of these videos demonstrate how teachers should encourage student thinking and give time for students to make sense of problems.

In this kindergarten video, students are working with red and yellow counters to find different combinations to make a ten. Watch the video and look for instances of how the students are interacting with the mathematics.

 www.solution-tree.com/Determining_Number_Pairs_for_Ten

Observe how the students make sense of the mathematics in the task and how the teacher uses questioning to engage students in thinking. In what ways do the representations students create help them make sense of the task? What does the teacher do to encourage flexible use of representations?

You will notice from the beginning of the video that students are using counters and drawing pictures to make sense of the problem. This approach is an important aspect of supporting students to solve problems; providing materials for the students to use as they attempt to make sense of the mathematics allows them to demonstrate application of Mathematical Practice 5, "Use appropriate tools strategically." Students use their tools in any way that makes sense to them. When the teacher circulates in the classroom, she asks students questions about their models and whether they used counters or drawings, and she encourages them to explain their answers by using their models. Notice how she questions the students, asking them to make connections between the counters, their drawings, and their number sentences.

Students will often err in their responses, sometimes from a lack of careful attention to their work, sometimes from a gap in their mathematical understanding. It is important for you to be able to diagnose the difference. Notice what the teacher in the video does when students make an error. Early on, a student identifies that 6 + 4 equals 8, and rather than correcting the student, the teacher asks him to use the counters to determine the sum. The student correctly counts and identifies that the total is 10. Not only has the student corrected his response, but he has also determined why 10 is the correct sum. In this way, the teacher allows the student to understand both the correct total and how to determine the total. Her approach supports student sense making and student responsibility for correcting errors. Later in the video, when recording number pairs to 10 on the board, one student contributes "10 = 4 + 8," and the teacher asks the students if this is a correct number sentence. She selects a different student who identifies that this is not correct and provides the correct number pair to 10. Notice how the teacher returns to the student who contributed the incorrect number pair to develop correct understanding. The student initially answers incorrectly, but with support, provides a correct number pair for 10. This is an important teacher move, supporting a student who presents an error indirectly by having other students provide successful strategies and allowing students to use those strategies to build their own understanding. It takes time and attention to unpack student thinking, and the teacher makes a conscious effort to guide the pathway of questioning in order to loop back to students who need support.

In this classroom, students are making sense of the problem as they work throughout the lesson to determine the correct sums to 10. What happens when students make errors? How does the teacher respond to students who make the correct sum? The teacher facilitates student thinking by asking them to explain their work and make sense of multiple answers for sums to 10. Students should understand the importance of persevering to make sense of both the problem and their answers. You can encourage this behavior when you ask students to explain their work, even when they are correct. This teacher pushes students to extend their thinking, regardless of the solutions, which is an example of how you can support Mathematical Practice 1, "Make sense of problems and persevere in solving them."

The teacher also demonstrates flexible use of the equal sign when she calls the class back and begins to write on the whiteboard. By starting each of her number sentences with "10 =," she is providing students with an example of how the total can be written on the left side of the number sentence. This is a purposeful teacher move where she chooses to represent the number pairs in a way that helps students maintain a flexible understanding of number sentences. In writing the 10 first, the teacher is working to provide examples that are different than the traditional format of a number plus a number is the sum, which can lead to the student misconception that the equal sign means "and the answer is . . .". By writing the number sentences in the manner that she does, she works to provide flexibility in student understanding of this important mathematical concept. She is also supporting them to engage in Mathematical Practice 4, "Model with mathematics."

In the second video, students are working with a word problem that models 7 + 8. Students use counters, ten frames, and whiteboards and markers to represent their thinking regarding adding these two quantities. Watch the video before reading on. As you watch, focus on the students. What strategies do students use to determine the answer? How does the student work connect to the students' understanding of the mathematics in the task?

www.solution-tree.com/Using_the_Make-a-Ten
_Strategy_With_Addition

The students use many different strategies to add these numbers. The first student in the small group begins the discussion with the teacher by identifying how he assigned each type of prize a different color counter, making sure that he is representing the problem accurately. He then presents his addition strategy as "counting all," where he includes all of the counters in determining the sum. The student places seven counters in one ten frame and eight counters in the other one. This indicates how this student is thinking about these values as separate and is not necessarily connecting how to use the ten frame to help organize his thinking about place value. While this is not an indication that the student cannot use this strategy, it does indicate that he is not representing it in this instance.

In the second round of small-group work, the first student demonstrates a decomposition strategy that allows her to make a ten by pulling out 5 from each of the two addends. Her diagram clearly represents her thinking and her ability to make a ten. This may not have been a strategy that you would predict a student would use, which illustrates that it is important to investigate the strategies and reasoning that were not anticipated in planning. You must consider all methods that students use and check to be sure that they are mathematically accurate.

Next, the teacher asks a student to explain another student's strategy, and she describes a different make-a-ten strategy. She discusses how 3 can be used from the 8, which when combined with 7, makes 10. As there are still 5 remaining from the 8 (she took 3 from it to make the 10), this is added to the 10 and gives a sum of 15.

The teacher notices that the other student in this group has 8 + 7 represented on her whiteboard, so she asks her for her strategy. At this point, you might expect to hear another fact strategy. However, the student describes how she added the two numbers and states that she "counted" to determine the sum of 15. Finally, the student who comes to the board in the later part of the task also uses a make-a-ten strategy to determine the sum. These strategies show how important the role of listening—for both learners and teachers—is to develop a deep understanding of mathematics.

TQE Process

At this point, it may be helpful to watch the second video again. Pay close attention to the tasks, questioning, and opportunities to collect evidence of student learning.

The TQE process can help you frame your observations. Teachers who have a deep understanding of the mathematics they teach:

- Select appropriate *tasks* to support identified learning goals

- Facilitate productive *questioning* during instruction to engage students in the Mathematical Practices

- Collect and use student *evidence* in the formative assessment process during instruction

The *task* in this lesson provides the opportunity to determine different ways that students add 7 + 8. While the learning goal focuses on the different strategies for adding to get a sum greater than 10, the task begins with a story problem. This allows the students to make sense of the addition problem in a meaningful way. By selecting the addends of 7 and 8, the teacher could expect many different strategies from the students, including counting all, counting on, make a ten, and doubles plus one. Selecting a task that supports the use of multiple strategies provides students the opportunity to engage in Mathematical Practice 7, "Look for and make use of structure." Understanding the value of grouping ones into tens foreshadows work with place value. The structure of place value is an important mathematical concept for students to grasp for later work with greater numbers.

The use of *questioning* in this lesson helps students deepen their understanding of the task. The teacher asks questions that are open ended so students can share their thinking. The teacher also uses wait time to allow students time to make sense of her questions, and she is patient when students provide explanations of their thinking. Some of the questions the teacher asks require students to provide more detail in their explanations. These questions help the teacher determine how well students are making sense of the task. When the teacher asks one student to explain how another student uses the ten frame, it allows the teacher to see how that student interprets a strategy different from her own work. This encourages students to learn the strategies that others are using. The teacher uses questions to focus on the learning goal, exploring different strategies for adding 7 and 8.

The teacher collects *evidence* of student learning throughout the lesson. Notice how the teacher listens carefully to each student response and often turns to another student to see if he or she understands the explanation. The teacher asks questions to probe student thinking, such as "Can you show me how you did that?" and has students explain other students' strategies by asking questions such as "Can you explain to me what you think she did?" The responses provide information about each student's level of understanding, and both questions and responses are important elements of an effective formative assessment process. In order to best support student understanding, be sure to have a clear picture of how each student makes sense of problems.

The Response

Students often make mistakes when adding or subtracting multidigit numbers. It is helpful to consider the basis of their mistakes. It may be procedural, conceptual, or both. Another consideration is whether students can decompose and compose numbers in meaningful ways. Students' early experiences breaking numbers apart provide practice for meaningful composition and decomposition of numbers later. How do the students work to make sense of addition and subtraction, and how do they use invented strategies to determine their answers? Students should be able to explain how and why their strategy works. If they struggle with these explanations, their difficulties may clarify where they need support in the learning progression. Gaps in understanding may come from a lack of balance between conceptual understanding and procedural fluency, so providing experiences in which students connect their thinking with multiple types of models and strategies alongside multiple word problem structures will provide help for all students.

When students have difficulty with addition and subtraction, the struggle may come from moving through the learning progression too quickly. Research has shown that when considering how to support students, teachers need to be cautious and not move to algorithms before students are ready (Stigler, Gonzales, Kawanaka, Knoll, & Serrano, 1999). Students need time in kindergarten through grade 2 to make sense of problems in their own way. They need to create their own solution pathways, compare them with other students, and then work to develop more efficient processes. Remember, the goal is not to just get the correct answers or to jump to the standard algorithm but to get the correct answers in a process that makes sense to the student. It is important for students to have the time they need to build depth of understanding—and the amount of time needed may not be the same for all students.

Reflections

1. What do you feel are the key points in this chapter?

2. What challenges might you face when implementing the key ideas from this chapter? How will you overcome them?

3. What important features help students develop an understanding of addition and subtraction using counting strategies, and how will you ensure your instruction embeds the support needed for these features?

4. Select a recent lesson you have taught or observed focused on addition or subtraction with counting strategies. Relate this lesson to the TQE process.

5. What changes will you make to your planning and instruction based on what you read and considered from this chapter?

CHAPTER 4

Addition and Subtraction Using Grouping Strategies

The key to obtaining procedural fluency is to begin with building conceptual understanding of addition and subtraction. Addition and subtraction contexts, along with visual models, aid in understanding the operations, which enables students to create self-invented strategies. In this chapter, you will explore invented strategies and a variety of standard algorithms with the purpose of supporting the development of computational fluency with multidigit addition and subtraction using grouping strategies. An important aspect of fluency is the ability to choose strategies that are most efficient for a given task. You will examine the progression of the standards related to obtaining this fluency alongside potential misconceptions by engaging with meaningful tasks. The initial task in this chapter begins with a candy shop context referred to in chapter 1. This context will assist in making sense of addition and subtraction procedures based on place value and properties of operations.

The Challenge

Complete the task in figure 4.1 using your knowledge that there are 10 pieces of candy in a roll and 10 rolls in a box.

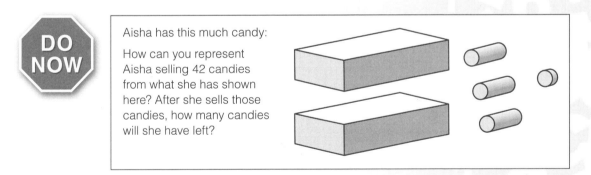

Aisha has this much candy:

How can you represent Aisha selling 42 candies from what she has shown here? After she sells those candies, how many candies will she have left?

Figure 4.1: Selling candies in the candy shop task.

When solving the task in figure 4.1, you may want to draw pictures and decide on how you would explain and justify your solution. What came to your mind when solving this problem? What approach did you use? As you re-examine your approach, consider how your understanding of place value helped you think about the task. Now think about how students might address this task. What type of errors do you anticipate students will make in solving it? The discussion that follows will be much more meaningful if you make an attempt to complete the task by using a picture and writing out your explanation.

The structure of how the candy is packaged matches the structure of the base ten number system. The task begins with 2 boxes, 3 rolls, and 1 piece. Selling 42 candies can be accomplished by selling 4 rolls and 2 pieces. There are not enough rolls to sell without unpacking a box. After unpacking a box, Aisha now has 1 box, 13 rolls, and 1 piece. Now you can sell 4 rolls, and that will leave you with 1 box, 9 rolls, and 1 piece (see figure 4.2).

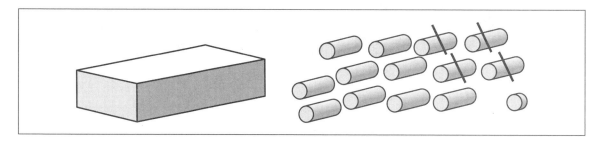

Figure 4.2: Selling candies in the candy shop—strategy one, step two.

The next step is to sell 2 pieces. However, you currently have only 1 piece of candy. In order to sell 2 pieces, you will need to unpack a roll; this will leave 1 box, 8 rolls, and 11 pieces. Now if you sell 2 pieces, you will be left with 1 box, 8 rolls, and 9 pieces (see figure 4.3), which is 189 candies.

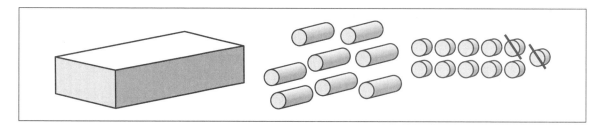

Figure 4.3: Selling candies in the candy shop—strategy one, step three.

Another way to approach this task is to set up your model to allow you to make all of the trades at once. If 42 candies have to be sold, then you need to be able to create a representation that includes 4 rolls and 2 pieces. In order to sell that number of candies, you will need to unpack a box and a roll; this will leave 1 box, 12 rolls, and 11 pieces. Now, there is enough of each type of package to sell 4 rolls and 2 pieces, leaving 1 box, 8 rolls, and 9 pieces (see figure 4.4).

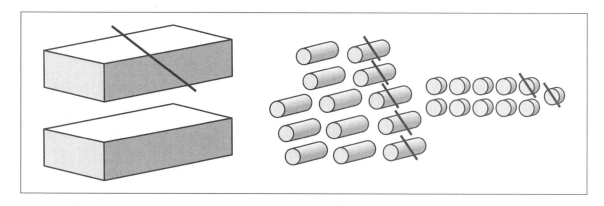

Figure 4.4: Selling candies in the candy shop—strategy two.

Which Mathematical Practice did you engage in for this task? Perhaps you used Mathematical Practice 7, "Look for and make use of structure." The structure is the ten-to-one relationship of pieces to rolls and rolls to boxes and being able to relate that understanding to place value. How is this task related to addition and subtraction procedures? In relation to the task in figure 4.1, either of the strategies detailed is correct and both are efficient.

The experience of unpacking boxes and rolls sets the stage and provides the reasoning for decomposing numbers for multidigit subtraction procedures where regrouping is required. Although not used in this particular task, the experience of *packing* boxes and rolls also sets the stage for composing numbers for multidigit addition procedures where regrouping is required. Particular strategies for addition and subtraction procedures will be discussed in The Mathematics section of this chapter (page 74). However, prior to examining strategies, it is important to examine a progression of the standards for developing addition and subtraction procedures based on place value and properties of operations.

The Progression

The development of addition and subtraction procedures in this book is determined by the belief that conceptual understanding must precede procedural fluency to build mathematical understanding and proficiency. Having procedural fluency means that you can identify and apply accurate, efficient, and generalizable ways of computing.

Procedural fluency with addition and subtraction builds on the foundation of a deep understanding of addition and subtraction using counting strategies, as discussed in chapter 3. Following is a progression for the development of addition and subtraction using grouping strategies.

- Add and subtract using grouping with objects and various models.

- Solve word problems involving addition and subtraction.

- Make sense of and apply properties of operations and the relationship between addition and subtraction.

- Explain that the two digits of a two-digit number represent amounts of tens and ones.

- Make sense of adding within 100 by adding tens to tens and ones to ones.

- Add and subtract within 1,000 using strategies, concrete models, or drawings based on place value, properties of operations, and the relationship between addition and subtraction.

The placement of topics across grades provides a lens on how content develops over time. As students progress from kindergarten to second grade, they develop more abstract ways of reasoning about addition and subtraction procedures. This foundation supports using the standard algorithms for addition and subtraction in grade 3. It is important that deep and meaningful connections are developed between the content at each grade level.

Here, we'll detail the progression at each grade level.

Kindergarten

At this grade level, students are developing a foundation for later exploration of place value by composing and decomposing numbers from 11–19 into 10 ones and some more ones. Just as with word problems, they use objects and drawings to represent these compositions and decompositions. The foundation of place value helps students invent strategies for adding and subtracting.

Grade 1

In terms of place value, grade 1 students begin to understand the composition of two-digit numbers as representing amounts of tens and ones. This is different from explorations in kindergarten where students think of numbers as 10 ones and some more ones, now the 10 ones are thought of as 1 ten. This is an important aspect of the progression of understanding from kindergarten to grade 1. This understanding extends to the addition of two-digit numbers by adding tens to tens and ones to ones. Given a two-digit number, students mentally find ten more or ten less, while also being able to subtract multiples of 10 from multiples of 10 using numbers in the range of 10–90, such as when solving 60 − 20. When adding and subtracting, grade 1 students continue to use concrete models or drawings as well as strategies based on place value and properties of operations. Additionally, students begin to explain their reasoning for solving addition and subtraction problems.

Grade 2

Grade 2 students add and subtract within 1,000, building on their fluency with adding and subtracting within 100, using various strategies involving place value, properties of operations, and the relationship between addition and subtraction. Using mental images, they fluently add and subtract within 20. Additionally, second-grade students mentally add or subtract 10 or 100 to a given number. They are able to explain why addition and subtraction strategies work using place value and the properties of operations.

Throughout this progression, the emphasis is on students' reasoning and sense making with addition and subtraction strategies based on place value and properties of operations. Initially, word problems provide the context for students to deepen their understanding of modeling with mathematics by generating models, drawings, and equations that represent situations. Through their engagement with word problems, students gain a personal connection with the context. Using the context to make sense of the operations enables them to create invented strategies for addition and subtraction. These strategies contribute to addition and subtraction procedures and later lead students to fluently use the standard algorithms for addition and subtraction.

Next, you will explore a variety of strategies for addition and subtraction based on the use of place value and grouping. The goal is to provide experiences that will allow you to solve problems in flexible ways, which provides the background to introduce these techniques to your students and lead discussions on the efficiency, convenience, or appropriateness of each strategy for various problems.

The Mathematics

As indicated in The Progression, sophisticated ways of reasoning about operations are developed over time through contextual problems and experiences related to the use of concrete models and drawings. This development is nurtured by opportunities to gain flexible computational skills through the use of tasks that build understanding of mental computation and other efficient ways to compute. While contextual problems were the focus of chapter 2, in this chapter you explore strategies for addition and subtraction procedures without context.

Using Strategies for Addition

There are several strategies and procedures—including base ten blocks, column addition, and the standard addition algorithm—that can be used to add multidigit numbers. However, base ten blocks provide a useful entry point into addition and subtraction using grouping strategies. Use base ten blocks to represent the addition problem provided in figure 4.5.

Use base ten blocks to add the following:

```
   1 4 9
 + 2 8 6
```

Figure 4.5: Multidigit addition task.

How did you use the blocks to act out the addition process? You could have combined hundreds first, then combined the tens, and lastly combined the ones. By doing this, you would have 3 hundreds, 12 tens, and 15 ones. You could then connect this process to your experience with packing candies in the candy shop to pack base ten blocks. For candies, the term *pack* is appropriate; however for base ten blocks, you might also use *trade* or *exchange*. You trade 10 tens for 1 hundred and 10 ones for 1 ten. This results in a sum of 4 hundreds, 3 tens, and 5 ones, or 435. Figure 4.6 (page 76) provides a model that represents the answer to this problem.

It is important to note that although this method does not match the standard algorithm for addition, it may match how you thought about your invented algorithm and is seen as a credible strategy.

Another strategy you could use with base ten blocks is to combine like blocks one at a time, starting with the ones. You are combining 9 ones with 6 ones, resulting in a total of 15 ones. With this strategy, 10 ones can be traded for 1 ten; as a result, 15 ones represent 1 ten and 5 ones. Next, you combine all the tens. Originally, there was a set of 4 tens and a set of 8 tens. After combing the ones, there is an additional ten, which results in a total of 13 tens. Now 10 tens can be traded for 1 hundred, so 13 tens represents 1 hundred and 3 tens. Initially, there was a set of 1 hundred and 2 hundreds; however, after combining the tens, there is an additional hundred, which results in a total of 4 hundreds. Figure 4.7 (page 77) documents the steps using this strategy to represent your answer to this problem.

Unlike the representation in figure 4.6, this method does match the steps of the standard algorithm. However, the use of traditional language for describing the standard algorithm does not describe this process. It is important to note that the word *carry* was not used. Rather, the word *trade* was used; *trading* matches the context of the task, as does *exchanging*. You are trading 10 ones for 1 ten. Figure 4.8 (page 78) displays the sequence of recording the steps as you progress through this strategy. Notice how this way of recording the steps resembles the traditional algorithm.

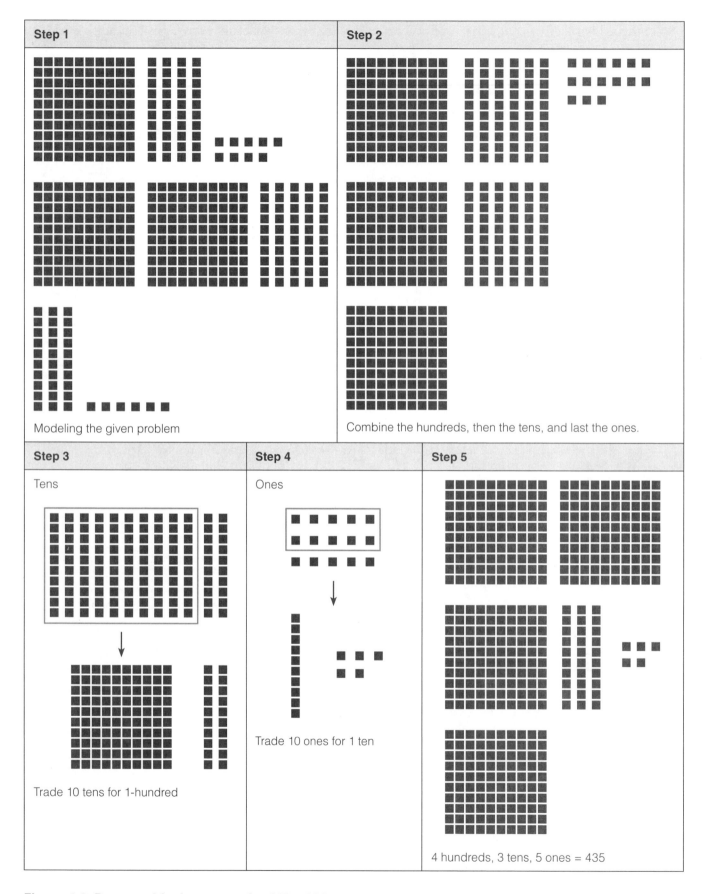

Figure 4.6: Base ten blocks answer for 149 + 286.

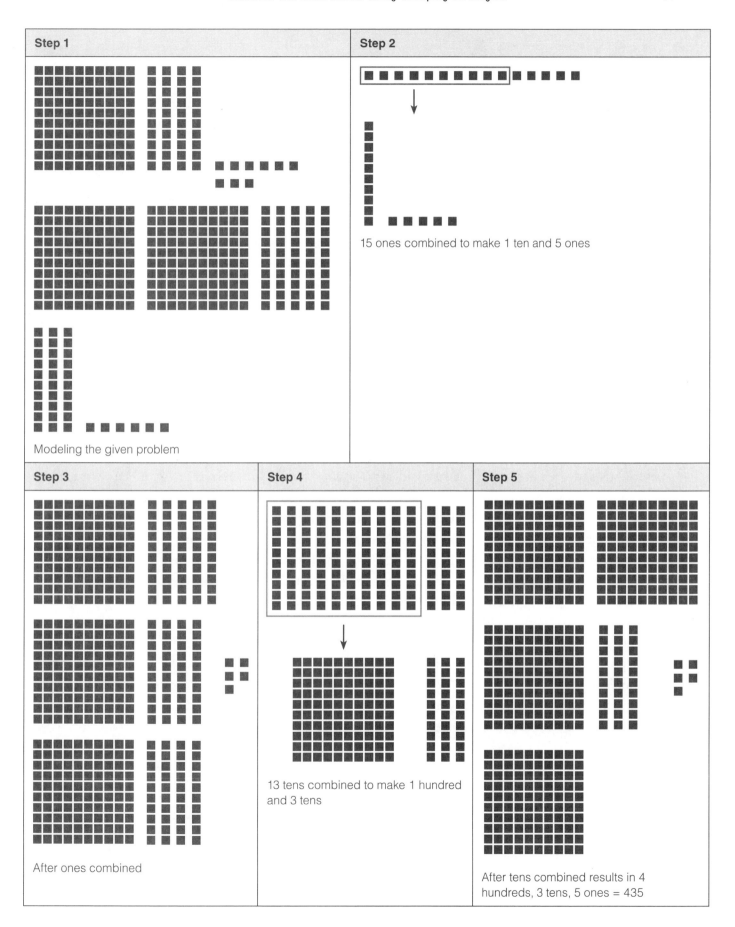

Figure 4.7: Second base ten blocks answer for 149 + 286.

1		1 1		1 1
149	→	149	→	149
+ 286		+ 286		+ 286
5		35		435

Figure 4.8: Recording the steps of the second base ten blocks solution strategy.

Using base ten blocks provides a concrete model with direct links to place value. This model helps you make sense of your invented strategy. A useful algorithm for connecting base ten blocks to place value is column addition.

For the column addition strategy, you write the problem on a place value chart. You record the values for each place in its own column. Figure 4.9 demonstrates this strategy.

Hundreds	Tens	Ones	
1	4	9	
+ 2	8	6	
3	12	~~15~~	
3	~~12~~	5	→ Trade 10 ones for 1 ten
4	3	5	→ Trade 10 tens for 1 hundred

Figure 4.9: Column addition strategy for 149 + 286.

Adding the ones results in a sum of 15 ones, written in the ones column; adding the tens results in a sum of 12 tens, written in the tens column; and lastly, adding the hundreds results in 3 hundreds, written in the hundreds column. After recording column sums, the next step is to determine whether trades need to be made. If so, you should make the trades below the first recorded entries, as indicated in figure 4.8. Many teachers have an issue with this approach, as two digits are recorded in one place, which often leads to a common error in multidigit addition. However, this is a common error with the traditional standard algorithm as well. Column addition may help students who make this error with the traditional standard algorithm focus on the process of regrouping and ultimately resolve the error on their own. The choice of column addition allows you to consider how to represent sums and place value in a careful and considered manner and possibly use this error as a springboard for learning. The trading is more explicit with this algorithm than with the standard algorithm, and so students are more likely to engage in Mathematical Practice 7, "Look for and make use of structure," when they see that every time there are two digits in a column, they must make a trade. When they make sense of this process, they will have more success with the standard algorithm.

It is very likely that you know the standard algorithm at a level that is automatic: this strategy has been engrained in your head, and you use it without thinking about why you carry. *Carry* sounds like it should be a good term to use since, on paper, the process looks like a value is "carried" from one place to another, but what does it *mean* to carry? Think about the mathematical action associated with the term. With this algorithm, the language you use is critical in making sense of the process. Before continuing, take some time to think about how to add 149 and 286 using the standard algorithm (see figure 4.10).

Write out the reasoning for each of your steps in using the standard algorithm to add 149 + 286.

Figure 4.10: Describing the standard algorithm for multidigit addition.

Do your written steps look similar to the following process? This process corresponds with how you may have been taught; however, there are many issues with these steps.

> Starting with the ones place, add 9 and 6. You get 15. Write the 5 in the ones column, and carry the 1 to the tens column. Write the 1 directly above the 4. Next, add the tens column. Eight plus 4 plus 1 is 13. Write the 3 in the tens column, and carry the 1 to the hundreds column. Write the 1 directly above the 1 in the hundreds column. And lastly, add the numbers in the hundreds column. One plus 2 plus 1 is 4. Write the 4 in the hundreds column. The answer is 435.

When referring to the previous strategies described for use with base ten blocks and column addition, we've continuously demonstrated appropriate use of place value language and understanding. In addition, every step within those strategies was mathematically sound. However, when unpacking *these* steps, the following set of statements is misleading and not mathematically sound.

- "You get 15. Write the 5 in the ones column, and carry the 1 to the tens column. Write the 1 directly above the 4."

- "Eight plus 4 plus 1 is 13. Write the 3 in the tens column, and carry the 1 to the hundreds column. Write the 1 directly above the 1 in the hundreds column."

In the first bullet, the 15 is separated into 5 and 1. Is it a one? No, it is 1 ten. Also, when the word *carry* is used, it implies that this so-called one is being taken someplace. It is not; it is still part of the same sum. The same inappropriate use of mathematics language is observed in the second bullet, but in addition to this, when 4, 8, and 1 are added to get 13, there is no indication that these are tens. Descriptions of the addition process such as these lead students to adopt inappropriate mathematics language and undo their understanding of place value. When teaching this strategy or any other strategy for addition and subtraction, it is imperative to apply Mathematical Practice 6, "Attend to precision." This practice must be observed in teachers first if there is any hope that it will be observed in students. Teachers must model careful and appropriate use of place value language.

When addressing steps used in the standard algorithm, it is important to refer to the digits in relation to their place value.

An appropriate way to write or explain these steps for the first bullet is:

> You get 15. That is 15 ones. Trade 10 ones for 1 ten, and then you will have 1 ten and 5 ones. Record the 1 ten above the tens column and the 5 ones in the answer space of the ones column.

Refer to figure 4.11 for the symbolic representation of this part of the process.

An appropriate way to write or explain these steps for the second bullet is:

> Eight plus 4 plus 1 is 13 tens. That is 13 tens. Trade 10 tens for 1 hundred, and then you will have 1 hundred and 3 tens. Record the 1 hundred above the hundreds column and the 3 tens in the answer space of the tens column.

Refer to figure 4.12 for the symbolic representation of this part of the process.

Think about the difference in each set of written steps. In the revised set of steps, the mathematics language is appropriate, and each step is mathematically sound. Compare the revised steps with the steps that describe the process of adding with base ten blocks. Think about how they are similar and how they are different.

```
    1
  1 4 9
+ 2 8 6
-------
      5
```

Figure 4.11: Representation to help explain the standard addition algorithm.

```
  1 1
  1 4 9
+ 2 8 6
-------
    3 5
```

Figure 4.12: Second representation to help explain the standard addition algorithm.

The standard addition algorithm should be introduced after students have had opportunities to explore and create invented strategies on their own. Because of the nature of this algorithm, students will not likely invent this strategy; so teachers will probably need to provide direct instruction on its use. This is an appropriate place for the gradual release of responsibility model: "I do, we do, you do," as described in the introduction so that the teacher first provides a demonstration of the standard addition algorithm, then engages the whole class in applying the algorithm, and finally allows students to work independent of the teacher to apply the algorithm. Note that this algorithm calls for regrouping, but—as noted previously—throughout this chapter, we refer to this process as trading, exchanging, or with the candy shop, packing. All of these words are appropriate. As the focus on computing shifts to subtracting in the next section, *trading* will describe the regrouping process.

Using Strategies for Subtraction

Subtracting whole numbers is often more difficult than adding. In this section, you will explore strategies to support the development of understanding the operation of subtraction, including the use of base ten blocks, flexible grouping, trade-first subtraction, and the standard subtraction algorithm.

In preparation for a discussion of using strategies, including the standard algorithm, to subtract multidigit numbers, use base ten blocks to represent the problem provided in figure 4.13.

There are multiple ways to subtract these numbers. You may decide to make both numbers with base ten blocks: 436 using 4 hundreds, 3 tens, and 6 ones, and 82 using 8 tens and 2 ones. In order to find the difference between the two numbers, you can proceed with matching the set of blocks to see what is left (see figure 4.14).

Figure 4.13: Multidigit subtraction task.

Number	Blocks to Represent Number	Unpack (Trade)	Difference
436			
82			

Figure 4.14: Base ten block representation of 436 – 82.

After starting to match the blocks, you realize that there are not enough tens represented for 436 to match the 8 tens in 82. As a result, you must trade 1 hundred from 436 for 10 tens. So, 436 is now represented as 3 hundreds, 13 tens, and 6 ones (see figure 4.15, page 82).

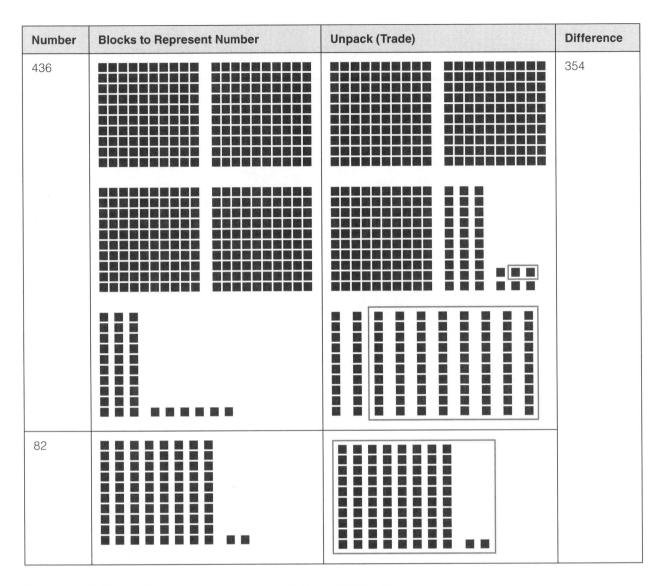

Number	Blocks to Represent Number	Unpack (Trade)	Difference
436			354
82			

Figure 4.15: Unpacking base ten representation of 436 – 82.

This trading is very similar to unpacking candies in chapter 1. The blocks inside the rectangles in the third column indicate the matching of the blocks. After matching blocks for 82 in both numbers, you can conclude that the difference between 436 and 82 is 354, represented by the blocks that are not inside the rectangle.

On the other hand, you could begin with blocks to represent 436 as 4 hundreds, 3 tens, and 6 ones. Rather than also representing 82 with blocks, you could decide to physically take 82 (8 tens, 2 ones) away from 436 (see figure 4.16). In doing so, you might realize that there are not enough tens represented in 436 to take 8 tens away. Therefore, you trade 1 hundred for 10 tens. This approach results in a representation showing 13 tens. After taking 8 tens and 2 ones away, there are 354 left represented as 3 hundreds, 5 tens, and 4 ones.

Both representations obtain the same answer but show different strategies. Comparing different representations and strategies creates opportunities to make sense of the work of others. This supports Mathematical Practice 3, "Construct viable arguments and critique the reasoning of others."

Number	Blocks to Represent Number	Take Away 82	Difference
436	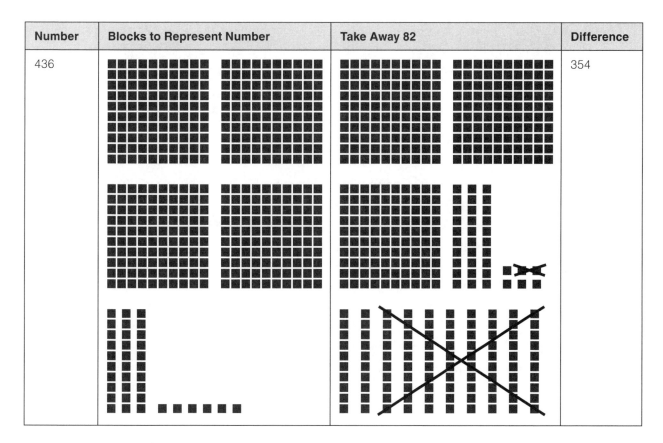		354

Figure 4.16: Second base ten representation of 436 – 82.

Another way to subtract is to use flexible grouping. This strategy requires a solid foundation in understanding place value, as you need to be flexible with the grouping of numbers. Recall the candy shop task in chapter 1 where you had to think of multiple ways to represent a number. For instance, 60 can be represented as 6 rolls, 5 rolls and 10 pieces, or even as 60 pieces. Consider the task in figure 4.11 (page 80), how many tens are in 436? Is it 3 or 43? There are 43 tens in 436. Another strategy for subtracting 82 from 436 is to think of 436 as tens and ones from the start. The number 436 can be thought of as 43 tens and 6 ones.

You can take 2 ones from 6 ones, leaving you with 4 ones. Record the 4 in the ones place. Now, you need to subtract 8 tens from 43 tens. This leaves you with 35 tens, which is the same as 3 hundreds and 5 tens (see figure 4.17).

Figure 4.17: Subtracting 436 – 82 using flexible grouping.

This strategy is known as flexible grouping because rather than thinking of 436 as 4 hundreds, 3 tens, and 6 ones, as is often the case, the number is grouped in more flexible ways, in this case as 43 tens and 6 ones. This strategy reinforces the understanding of place value. Consider the problem in figure 4.18. Complete the subtraction problem using flexible grouping prior to reading on.

Figure 4.18: Multidigit subtraction task.

You may see 203 as 20 tens and 3 ones. In order to subtract 8 ones from 3 ones in this problem, it is still necessary to regroup. However, now, rather than needing to determine how to regroup with a zero, you need only to regroup 20 tens as 19 tens and 10 ones, so you have 19 tens and 13 ones. Now you can subtract 8 ones from 13 ones to get 5 ones and 6 tens from 19 tens to get 13 tens for a solution of 135. Is this how you solved it?

Take some time and think about how you would talk someone else through the problem using the standard subtraction algorithm. How would you describe changing 203 to 1 hundred, 9 tens, and 13 ones? Hopefully, you would not attempt to "borrow" or worse, "borrow sugar from next door." Occasionally, grade 2 teachers use this language to explain subtraction. Teachers might say, "You can't subtract 8 from 3, so you have to go next door to borrow sugar. But no one is home, so you have to go to the next house." This type of storytelling will lead to considerable place value errors and does not support mathematical understanding. When the teacher "goes next door to borrow sugar," does he or she indicate that the house next door is ten times as large as the house in the ones place? Furthermore, the house in the hundreds place must be one hundred times as large as the house in the ones place! A more efficient way to approach this particular problem is to use the flexible grouping strategy. It supports an in-depth understanding of place value. However, even if the standard algorithm is used, proper place value language must be modeled in the solution process. Mathematical Practice 6, "Attend to precision," is reinforced in completing this problem using appropriate place value language. Additionally, Mathematical Practice 7, "Look for and make use of structure," is supported as you make use of the structure of the ten-to-one relationship of place value.

Trade-first subtraction is a strategy similar to the standard subtraction algorithm; however, all trades are conducted prior to subtracting. Refer to figure 4.19.

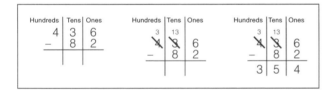

Figure 4.19: Trade-first strategy for 436 – 82.

This strategy is connected to the base ten block strategy (figure 4.13, page 81) with the exception that all the trades necessary with the blocks are made prior to performing any of the subtractions. In the trade-first strategy, the problem is placed into a place value table. Begin by trading in each column where there is not enough to take away, as shown in figure 4.19. There are enough ones to take 2 ones away; however, there are not enough tens represented to take 8 tens away. As a result, trade 1 hundred for 10 tens, which will give you a total of 13 tens, leaving 3 hundreds. Once all trades have been made, execute the problem, resulting in 3 hundreds, 5 tens, 4 ones, which is 354. Use of this strategy supports understanding of the standard algorithm. Notice how the language did not indicate that "you could not subtract 8 from 3" but rather that there were not enough tens to subtract 3 tens from 8 tens. This is because you *can* subtract 8 from 3—you will get –5; however, that is not a typical process for elementary mathematics. This is another example of attending to precision with proper use of language when describing mathematical procedures.

The approach to developing understanding of the standard subtraction algorithm is the same as the standard addition algorithm. As this strategy is developed, the reasoning for each step should be recorded. An important aspect of this strategy, as with any strategy, is attending to the use of appropriate place value language. A general way for explaining steps of the process is shown in figure 4.20.

This algorithm reinforces the use of base ten blocks. It connects the concrete strategy to a more abstract strategy. The process of recording each step—and the reasoning for each step—is crucial to understanding this strategy. Another crucial part of this algorithm is the use of appropriate place value language. That is why teachers should introduce this strategy with models, such as base ten blocks or candy shop pieces, to reinforce the language.

The learning progression for understanding addition and subtraction procedures evolves from developing skill in counting and cardinality to using direct modeling and counting strategies to add and subtract. Counting strategies move from those based on counting by ones to those that involve making and counting tens. Eventually, procedures involving place value are understood and used to add and subtract multidigit numbers, moving from counting tens, and making tens to operations based in place value. Students adopt their own ways of reasoning, and invented strategies become the foundation of understanding the standard algorithms.

The Classroom

Now that you have explored your own thinking related to addition and subtraction procedures, take a look into the classroom. In the first video, grade 2 students are applying addition procedures as they make sense of a word problem. The second video provides an extension to the importance of using proper place value as the teacher explores place value with decimals in a grade 5 class. Before you proceed, watch the video of the grade 2 class and look for instances of how the students engage in the mathematics task. As you watch, consider how the teacher prompts the students to make sense of the problem. How do the students engage in the task? What tools or strategies are the students using to model the task? How does the teacher use questioning to engage students in thinking about their thought processes?

1. Beginning with the ones place, I can take 2 ones from 6 ones, leaving 4 ones. I will record my answer in the ones answer column.

$$
\begin{array}{r}
4\ 3\ 6 \\
-\quad 8\ 2 \\
\hline
4
\end{array}
$$

2. In the tens column, there are not enough tens to take away 8 tens, so I need to trade 1 hundred for 10 tens, leaving 3 hundreds and 13 tens.

$$
\begin{array}{r}
3\ \ 13 \\
4\ 3\ 6 \\
-\quad 8\ 2 \\
\hline
4
\end{array}
$$

3. Now that I have enough tens, I can take 8 tens away from 13 tens, leaving 5 tens. I will record my answer in the tens answer column.

$$
\begin{array}{r}
3\ \ 13 \\
\cancel{4}\ \cancel{3}\ 6 \\
-\quad 8\ 2 \\
\hline
5\ 4
\end{array}
$$

4. And since there are no hundreds to take away, I will record a 3 in the hundreds answer column. The answer is 354.

$$
\begin{array}{r}
3\ \ 13 \\
\cancel{4}\ \cancel{3}\ 6 \\
-\quad 8\ 2 \\
\hline
3\ 5\ 4
\end{array}
$$

Figure 4.20: The standard subtraction algorithm strategy for 436 – 82.

www.solution-tree.com/Solving_a_Change_Unknown
_Word_Problem_With_Multidigit_Numbers

You will notice that from the beginning of the video, the teacher assists the students with processing the word problem.

> Jack buys a pencil and an eraser. The pencil costs 48 cents. The total cost for both the pencil and eraser is 73 cents. How much did the eraser cost?

Before attempting to solve a problem, students must understand what information is given as well as what the problem is asking them to do. When prompted by the teacher, the students unpack the word problem. After doing so, the students begin figuring out how to solve the problem by making use of the materials at their tables. Some of them use base ten blocks, the hundred chart, or whiteboards for representations. Providing various materials for students to use also supports the practice of making sense of the problem. These materials enable students to engage in Mathematical Practice 5, "Use appropriate tools strategically."

In this video, the students engage in making sense of their classmates' reasoning strategies. When this happens, students learn from each other and become flexible thinkers. The teacher facilitates this by asking a student to describe how her classmate used the hundred chart to arrive at the answer of 25. This teacher move supports students engaging in Mathematical Practice 3, "Construct viable arguments and critique the reasoning of others." Students learn from one another when they consider how the strategies of other students compare to their own. The teacher also demonstrates this practice when he gathers the class back as a whole group. He poses an incorrect reasoning strategy to the class. He states, "I heard someone solve the problem by adding the two numbers together and coming up with 121 cents. How many people agree with that?" This is a deliberate teacher move to engage students in critiquing the reasoning of others as well as to provide access to another strategy. Although the strategy is not correct, it provides an opportunity for students to compare their own strategies with others.

When selecting a student to share a different answer and strategy, the teacher returns to the student he was working with during small-group instruction. The purpose for selecting this student is to highlight the hundred chart strategy. This is also a deliberate practice and application of layers of facilitation (I facilitate the whole class, I facilitate small groups, I facilitate individuals) to provide a desired strategy for the students. When students are working in small groups, you should observe the strategies of all the students. During this time, you can be selective about what strategies you want students to observe in whole-class instruction.

After the student shares the hundred chart strategy, the teacher in the video asks another student to explain her thinking in relation to the context of the problem. Notice how the teacher responds to the student's statements with questions. The teacher asks, "Who knows why she started at 48?" Initially, the student states it was because 48 is the number of pencils. Right away, the teacher replies, "Is that how many pencils we have?" Here the teacher is supporting student engagement in Mathematical Practice 6, "Attend to precision." It is important that the student corrects herself in saying that 48 is the cost of the pencil instead of the number of pencils. Next, the teacher continues to support the student to make sense of the hundred chart strategy by having the student explain the answer of 25 when stopping at the 73 on the hundred chart. The teacher's questioning assists the student in making sense of the answer.

Throughout the video, the teacher does not give information as to whether a student is right or wrong. The teacher prompts the student to reflect on his or her own thinking. The teacher engages the students in metacognition. He supports students' sense making and responsibility for correcting errors. This can be difficult for teachers because at times, there is a natural urge to respond to a question without knowing exactly what a student is actually asking, thinking, or trying to say. It is important to allow the time necessary for students to complete their explanations. Through this technique of prompting, students are able to successfully demonstrate their reasoning strategy and answer their own questions.

Now turn your attention to a grade 5 class where the focus is on making sense of place value with decimals by representing decimals using base ten blocks. As you watch the video, pay close attention to the similarities and differences between how base ten blocks represent whole numbers versus decimals as well as to how language is used to make sense of place value. Before you proceed, watch the video and notice the ways in which students support their thinking.

www.solution-tree.com/Using_Place_Value
_Understandings_to_Model_Decimals

How are base ten blocks used differently to represent decimals? With whole numbers, the small cube is the unit. With decimals, the unit varies. In the first problem, students represent 1.34 by assigning the flat as the unit. Then, the rods are the tenths and the small cubes are hundredths. In the last problem, the large cube is the unit. Why can't 1.236 be represented using base ten blocks with the flat as the unit? This is because there is not a block to represent the thousandths, since the small cube is the smallest block. How do the students explain this?

They note the relationship between the blocks using appropriate place value language. The teacher questions them to help them focus on the ten-to-one relationship between thousandths and the hundredths, between hundredths and tenths, and so on. By supporting this focus during instruction, the teacher is supporting students to engage in Mathematical Practice 7, "Look for and make use of structure," in much the same way second-grade students make sense of place value but with whole numbers.

TQE Process

At this point, it may be helpful to watch the first video again (page 85). Pay close attention to the tasks, questioning, and opportunities to collect evidence of student learning.

The TQE process can help you frame your observations. Teachers who have a deep understanding of the mathematics they teach:

- Select appropriate *tasks* to support identified learning goals

- Facilitate productive *questioning* during instruction to engage students in the Mathematical Practices

- Collect and use student *evidence* in the formative assessment process during instruction

The learning goal of this *task* is to model and solve an addition word problem. One of the important features of choosing this task is that there are many ways to solve it. Some students may use counting on (as seen in the video with the hundred chart), counting back, a number line, base ten blocks, or trade-first subtraction. When you provide students with a task like this that can be solved in many ways, they have the opportunity to deepen their understanding of the structure of place value. In this lesson, the focus is on one technique, counting on. Students would have benefitted from seeing other strategies to solve the problem and connecting those strategies together. Developing understanding of place value is supported in this task as students have choice regarding what tools they can use, supporting students' engagement in Mathematical Practice 5, "Use appropriate tools strategically." In working to make sense of each other's reasoning, the students are participating in Mathematical Practice 3, "Construct viable arguments and critique the reasoning of others."

The *questioning* that the teacher uses throughout the lesson asks students to share their thinking. When a student shares how she is making sense of the task using a hundred chart, the teacher asks follow-up questions to unpack the student's understanding. The student is seeking to validate her strategy and solution. Notice how the teacher responds. Instead of telling her she is on the right path, he continuously asks the student to show what she means. It is apparent that she is using the counting on strategy; however, she has an incorrect solution. As a result, the teacher continues to prompt her to demonstrate her reasoning strategy using the hundred chart. This persistence in teacher questioning is important in order to have the student explain her strategy so that the teacher can be sure that he is not making an assumption about what the student understands. The teacher also encourages students to make sense of the strategies of other students. This approach supports students being flexible in their thinking; they learn the strategies that others are using and consider how their strategies connect with what other students are doing. This is another way to think of Mathematical Practice 3, "Construct viable arguments and critique the reasoning of others."

Throughout the lesson, the teacher collects *evidence* of the level of student understanding. The teacher listens carefully to students and asks questions to probe student understanding of the task. The questions that the teacher asks, and how he learns about the understanding of different students in the classroom, are important components of the formative assessment process. When the teacher shares an incorrect answer and strategy ("Someone solved the problem by adding together the two numbers and coming up with 121 cents"), he is probing for how many students considered addition instead of subtraction. He does not linger on this strategy but uses it as a springboard for considering other approaches and for connecting to the correct solution. As there were students who identified this as a correct process, it might have been appropriate to go deeper into the addition strategy and help students make sense of the proper operation in the context of this problem.

If a learning goal was for students to use grouping strategies to solve this problem, some students did not meet it. The teacher did not collect evidence of this thinking process from the student who shared. Perhaps the lack of using this strategy had something to do with the task or with where students were along the progression of making sense of multidigit addition and subtraction.

In order to best support student understanding, you need to know how the students make sense of the problems. This will provide you with the foundation to support growth along the learning progression of addition and subtraction procedures.

The Response

Students often make mistakes when using the standard algorithms for addition and subtraction. With addition problems, they forget to include the composed ten or hundred when a two- or three-digit addition problem is presented vertically. When a two-digit addition problem is presented horizontally, you might notice that students will add the ones digit of the first addend to the tens digit of the second addend. In subtraction, students take the smaller digit from the larger digit, no matter what order they are in the problem. Many times it will appear that students have not yet memorized their addition and subtraction facts. How should you address these needs? When a student experiences difficulty, it is important for the student to share his or her thinking so that the teacher is able to accurately identify the source of the difficulty with the student's understanding of place value.

Students need to have a strong foundation of place value. Errors may arise when students are not given enough opportunities to build number sense and operation sense through models and contextual situations. When students struggle with using the standard addition and subtraction algorithms, they will often benefit from returning to concrete experiences and work forward to build reasoning for the steps in the process. As you experienced via the tasks in this chapter, reasoning for the steps in the algorithm can be justified through the use of concrete representations. Multiple and varied experiences support students' ability to reason with numbers and operations in a way that is related to their lives. By providing opportunities for students to explore numbers and operations through context and models, students gain fluency and the ability to create and invent their own mathematical strategies.

During learning opportunities, instruction must engage students in the Mathematical Practices as they support mathematically proficient students. Specific to addition and subtraction procedures, students, along with their teachers, must attend to precision, which is Mathematical Practice 6. Using the appropriate language is crucial to students' understanding of operations and place value. Additionally, providing opportunities for students to create and share invented strategies with their peers supports Mathematical Practice 3, "Construct viable arguments and critique the reasoning of others." It is good for students to reason out strategies that they share with peers as they work to increase their flexible ways of thinking. However, it is also important to note that when creating and sharing strategies, students should be required to explain and justify the processes they use. Strategies should not be used without understanding, so explanation is key. Invented strategies help students make sense of mathematics. And lastly, Mathematical Practice 7, "Look for and make use of structure," is important in making sense of the place value relationship, which is the basis of the standard algorithms for addition and subtraction. Planning with these Mathematical Practices in mind will help address common errors in addition and subtraction procedures.

Reflections

1. What do you feel are the key points in this chapter?

2. What challenges might you face when implementing the key ideas from this chapter? How will you overcome them?

3. What are the important features for developing an understanding of addition and subtraction using grouping strategies, and how will you ensure your instruction embeds the support needed for these features?

4. Select a recent lesson you have taught or observed focused on addition or subtraction with grouping strategies. Relate this lesson to the TQE process.

5. What changes will you make to your planning and instruction based on what you read and considered from this chapter?

CHAPTER 5

Geometry

The focus of this chapter is the mathematics for teaching plane and solid geometry with depth so that you and your students develop a strong foundation for the study of geometry. What you need to know about the study of geometry is well beyond what you will address with K–2 students. This is in large part to ensure that you do not teach rules that will expire as students learn geometry in later grades.

Geometry is the study of space, objects in space, and the movement of objects in space. School geometry includes a focus on objects with zero, one, two, and three dimensions. Consider the images in figure 5.1.

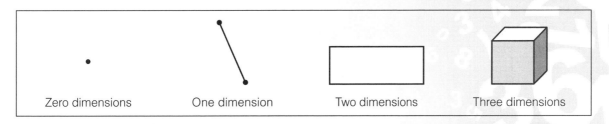

Figure 5.1: Dimensions of plane and solid geometry.

An example of an object with zero dimensions is a *point*. A point does not have dimensions such as length, width, and height. Although the geometric object of a point seems very simple, the point is quite vital to the subsequent dimensions in geometry. For instance, it takes two distinct points to create a line segment. A line segment is an example of an object with one dimension; it has length. By connecting line segments that do not exist on the same line, you can create objects with two dimensions, such as a rectangle. A rectangle has the dimensions of length and width. Zero-, one-, and two-dimensional geometry (commonly described as *plane geometry*) are abstract representations of the real world. When you hold up an attribute block that is the shape of a rectangle and say, "This two-dimensional shape is a rectangle," you are not actually correct. The shape you are holding is actually three-dimensional because it has length, width, and height to it. Even when you draw a representation of a rectangle on a sheet of paper, the drawn lines have a thickness, even though it is quite small. It is understood, by most adults, that you are ignoring the third dimension, the height, in order to represent the rectangle in a way that makes sense in the real world.

The question becomes, how do you truly represent two-dimensional objects in a three-dimensional world? Since students use screens constantly, you can represent objects correctly by referring to them on a TV, computer, or smartphone. As for the three-dimensional world (described as *solid geometry*), students are surrounded by it. The combination of these two worlds affords students the opportunity to explore concrete objects and helps provide models that represent the abstract objects of zero-, one-, and two-dimensional geometry, which will build toward three-dimensional geometry. Hereafter, two- and three-dimensional objects are referred to as shapes.

The Challenge

You can expect that K–2 students need a variety of tasks in order to acquire conceptual understanding in both plane (two-dimensional) and solid (three-dimensional) geometry. We designed the initial task in figure 5.2 to initiate a conversation about foundational principles for studying plane and solid geometry. This task is designed to provide you experience with the type of activities that your students need in order to use the language of geometry and develop a sense of space, both in two and three dimensions. While some of the expectations are beyond the kindergarten to grade 2 band, it is important for you to have the knowledge of the language and expectations in order to properly prepare your students for their next steps.

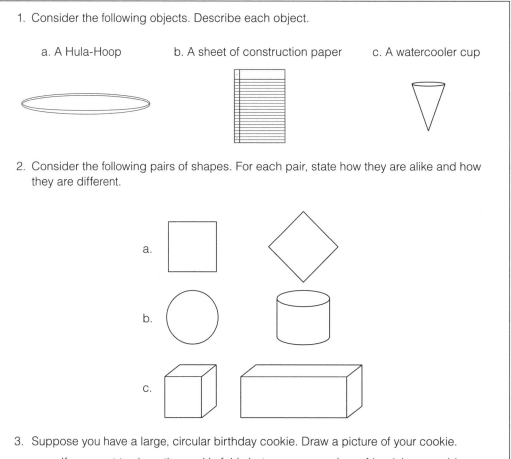

1. Consider the following objects. Describe each object.

   a. A Hula-Hoop   b. A sheet of construction paper   c. A watercooler cup

2. Consider the following pairs of shapes. For each pair, state how they are alike and how they are different.

   a.

   b.

   c.

3. Suppose you have a large, circular birthday cookie. Draw a picture of your cookie.

   a. If you want to share the cookie fairly between you and one friend, how would you cut the cookie? Draw a picture.

   b. If you want to share the cookie fairly between you and two friends, how would you cut the cookie? Draw a picture.

   c. If you want to share the cookie fairly between you and three friends, how would you cut the cookie? Draw a picture.

Figure 5.2: Geometry context task.

The first problem in the task in figure 5.2 relates to the importance of students learning to make observations about the environment and objects in their environment. Space is geometry's environment. You want students to be able to transfer their observation activity in the natural environment to observation activity in geometry's environment. Recall how you described a Hula-Hoop. Perhaps you included statements similar to the following.

- A Hula-Hoop is perfectly round.

- A Hula-Hoop is plastic.

- A Hula-Hoop has no ending or beginning.

- A Hula-Hoop has a hole in the middle.

- A Hula-Hoop looks like a big bracelet.

You might have also included things a Hula-Hoop can or cannot do. For instance, you might have stated that a Hula-Hoop can roll and it can be placed around other objects. Now, recall how you described a piece of notebook paper. Perhaps you included statements similar to the following.

- A sheet of notebook paper has three holes on the side.

- A sheet of notebook paper has lines on it.

- The lines on a sheet of notebook paper go from left to right (horizontal).

- A sheet of notebook paper is shaped like a rectangle.

- The lines on notebook paper are blue.

You might have also included things that a sheet of notebook paper can do or what can be done to it. For example, you might have included that a sheet of notebook paper can be folded in half. This sort of observation supports future understanding of fractions and symmetry.

Finally, recall your descriptions of a refrigerator; you may have included the following.

- A refrigerator is big.

- The doors of a refrigerator have handles.

- The doors of the refrigerator are shaped like rectangles.

- A refrigerator is taller than it is wide.

- A refrigerator comes in a box that is shaped just like the refrigerator.

You might have also included things that a refrigerator can do, such as keep food cold.

When students engage in considering how to describe these real-world objects, they link geometry concepts with their world. This engagement enables you to gather knowledge about the geometry concepts your students have already been exposed to through informal or formal geometry experiences, providing a lens on geometry topics students are ready to explore further as they develop their observation skills. For example, a student who says that the Hula-Hoop is perfectly round has perception about the uniformity of the shape and is able to translate his or her observations to reasonable descriptions. The student's use of vocabulary such as *round* is helpful in developing the foundation for early understanding of the shape of a circle. The examples in this task can help anchor students' understanding of a variety of geometry shapes.

Deep explorations in geometry will engage students in discussions about descriptions that are meaningful to learning geometry. For instance, a student who says a Hula-Hoop is pretty is making a subjective statement; the next student who describes a Hula-Hoop might not perceive it as pretty. Engaging students in making observations about the world around them and collecting their descriptions is a way to engage all students in the study of geometry.

The second problem in the geometry context task presents another important foundational concept to studying geometry—that of making comparisons. To compare shapes, you need to apply your observation and description skills. What do you notice about the first pair of shapes? Perhaps you see that they both have four sides and are the same size. How would you name them? You would probably be quick to say that the first shape looks like a square, but what about the second shape? Students often call this shape a diamond; however, it also looks like a square—it is the same as the first shape, but it has been rotated, or turned. Making comparisons also provides an opportunity to consider how shapes share common characteristics. It is important to ensure that differences are geometrically significant. A rotated or reflected (flipped) shape will still be named the same as a shape that is in a more common orientation, like the first square in figure 5.2 (page 92). Comparisons also provide a basis for developing definitions that include necessary distinctions, and this groundwork with shapes can happen with students even before they know the names of the shapes.

Consider your work on the third task in figure 5.2. Be sure you provided drawings to support your work. In this task, you should have considered how many people in total were to share the cookie. When students first read or hear this task, they sometimes neglect to do this and just share the cookie among the targeted friends. Also, when students work through this task, guide them away from spending too much time decorating and drawing the cookie. While this is an element of the task, it is not the primary goal. What you should have is three drawings similar to those in figure 5.3.

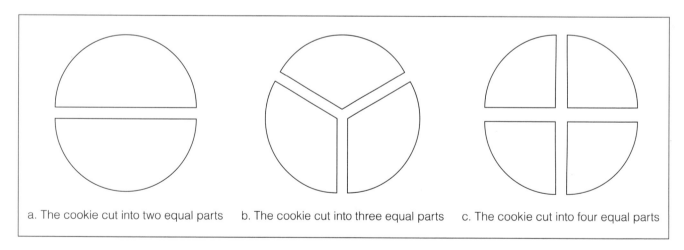

a. The cookie cut into two equal parts   b. The cookie cut into three equal parts   c. The cookie cut into four equal parts

Figure 5.3: Sharing a birthday cookie equally.

You can expect that some might falter on the "equalness" of the parts; be as exact as possible in order to develop this early understanding of a whole divided into equal parts as the foundation for fraction understanding. The use of a circular model for this early entry into fraction understanding is very common, but the idea can also be easily addressed with a rectangular model. In grade 1, the focus might be on halves and fourths. However, in grade 2, the focus will include thirds, and in grade 3, there is an expectation to use fraction notation and language for ⅓. The summary point is to use this geometry task to support work with fractions.

The Progression

Students' engagement in geometry tasks and activities greatly impacts their understanding of geometry. Geometry incorporates a variety of mathematics concepts allowing students to count the number of sides, angles, faces, and vertices of a shape, as well as measure attributes of a shape such as the length of sides. Students should be able to estimate to compare the length of sides of two shapes. Additionally, geometry is related to fraction understanding, and it is also a foundation for higher levels of mathematics, such as trigonometry.

The building of fraction concepts begins in early grades when students divide rectangles and circles in halves, thirds, and fourths as well as understanding that the more equal pieces a shape is divided into, the smaller the size of each piece. In trigonometry, unit circles and right-triangle geometry are used to calculate trigonometric ratios such as sine, cosine, and tangent. Hence, the geometry understanding students develop in K–2 is very important to students' overall mathematics learning. Following is a progression of geometry content through grade 2.

- Describe, analyze, and compare attributes of shapes.
- Identify and name shapes.
- Relate shapes to one another.
- Create and compose shapes.
- Classify shapes.

Here, we'll detail the progression at each grade level.

Kindergarten

Kindergarteners should spend significant time exploring geometry within the context of the environment in which they live. There are myriad shapes and objects in the environment that you can point out for students to notice, and you can provide scaffolding for students to begin developing the skill of describing what they can see or touch. As kindergarteners engage in formal learning opportunities and play, they use their language to share what they think or know about shapes and objects and their positions in the environment. Many childhood games, nursery rhymes, and songs can be incorporated to help students learn concepts important for geometry understanding. For example, Duck, Duck, Goose is played in a circle, "The Hokey Pokey" is a precursor for teaching students about position and movement (for example, *in, right, left, turn around*) of objects, and hopscotch is played on a diagram composed of squares. These opportunities allow you to use geometry language during young students' learning and play experiences.

Kindergarten geometry introduces students to naming and identifying two- and three-dimensional shapes like triangles, circles, squares, rectangles, rhombuses, trapezoids, other named polygons (such as pentagons and hexagons), cubes, right rectangular prisms, right circular cylinders, spheres, and cones.

Concrete models of these shapes should be easily accessible to students and should be used in a variety of ways so that students build strong familiarity with the shapes and are able to identify and name them.

Finally, kindergarteners begin to create their own models of shapes by drawing, folding paper, cutting paper, and even molding shapes from clay. The exactness of the model might not be in place, but the early understanding of the shapes reflected in the students' models will be helpful in assessing students' understanding of shapes' attributes.

Grade 1

Grade 1 geometry builds heavily on experiences from kindergarten. For instance, it is expected that as students' general-language and mathematics-language skills mature, their command of geometry vocabulary will be stronger and more formal. Grade 1 students use more refined definitions that include the essential attributes necessary for a mathematically powerful definition.

Composing and decomposing shapes is also an important experience in grade 1 geometry. At this grade level, students use several tools—pattern blocks, attribute blocks, construction paper—and develop the ability to use two or more shapes to compose a new shape. Some of this effort should involve visualization so that students begin developing an abstract perspective of composing shapes.

Grade 2

In grade 2, students build on geometry experiences from kindergarten and grade 1. That said, more specificity is required in grade 2 geometry. Geometry vocabulary increases with the inclusion of terms like *angles*, *parallel*, and *faces*. Students' ability to identify, create, and compose shapes strengthens in grade 2. Moreover, grade 2 geometry provides an opportunity to begin an early entry into understanding fractions by decomposing a shape into parts of equal sizes representing halves, thirds, and fourths although there is not an expectation for students to use fraction notation to record the fractions.

Grade 3

In grade 3, students use their geometry understandings from kindergarten through grade 2 to focus more clearly on classes of shapes. In addition, students' understanding of measurement provides a context for them to consider measurements related to the various shapes, such as the area and perimeter of select polygons.

Throughout this progression, the emphasis is on students' reasoning about shapes and their attributes. As students deepen their understanding of geometric concepts, students are better positioned to reason about geometry. Throughout this chapter, you will engage in multiple geometric tasks. At times, the content may go beyond grade 2; however, it is important to know the progression of the content.

The Mathematics

The following tasks highlight the important geometry content and important actions needed to fully experience geometry. These tasks become richer and more beneficial in an environment where you have the opportunity to work collaboratively by engaging in discourse and debate. Consider flexible ways of thinking since many of the tasks can have more than one correct or appropriate response. In this section, you should work through these tasks to explore the content and the mathematics actions that will engage students in the study of geometry. Here, you will explore understanding nondefining and defining attributes; relating attributes of shapes; sorting, defining, and classifying two-dimensional shapes; and recognizing three-dimensional shapes.

Understanding Nondefining and Defining Attributes

In geometry, it is valuable to observe and examine. When students study two-dimensional and three-dimensional geometry, they should observe, touch, hold, and rotate objects and concrete models of geometric shapes. Noticing shapes and their location, positioning, and size is a foundation for studying them in a formal learning environment. In addition, observing and examining objects provides the opportunity to use language, both formal and informal, to *describe* what is noticed. Increased exposure with objects and prompts for describing helps students develop more precise and clear language for what they notice when examining an object. For example, in the task in figure 5.4, you will use a collection of buttons. You may collect buttons from your personal belongings or purchase a set of assorted buttons from an arts and craft store. This informal task allows you to draw on your personal experiences, which support the development of your understanding of geometry.

Use a bag of twenty-five to thirty assorted buttons—varied in size, style, color, number of holes, and so on.

1. Sort the buttons.

2. Make a train of buttons so that each car or button in the train shares exactly one attribute with the car behind it and exactly one attribute with the car in front of it.

3. Make a train of buttons so that each car or button shares exactly two attributes with the car behind it and exactly two attributes with the car in front of it.

4. Make a train of buttons so that each car or button shares no attributes with the car behind it and no attributes with the car in front of it.

Figure 5.4: Attribute train task.

How did you do? You may have struggled at first to build the button trains, but perhaps the process to think about the button attributes became more familiar as you continued the task. The attribute train task brings observation, examination, and description together because in order to arrange the buttons, you need to observe the buttons, handle them, and develop a sorting method. The first level of the task is an open, unguided sorting activity. It addresses the notion that in geometry, you have to think flexibly and figure out more than one way of sorting shapes based on the context. This is why there isn't any guidance given for the sort. How did you sort the buttons? In other words, what rules did you create and use to sort the buttons? Your rules dictated the result of your sort, but the rules may or may not be similar to rules others might use.

Additionally, the open sort provides important information about what you are noticing in the process of sorting the buttons. For instance, you might find that initially you attempted to sort the buttons only by the attribute or characteristic of color. This can be a valuable and productive first step of sorting and one that is most often first chosen by students. However, it is important to note that color is a nondefining attribute in geometry. This is not the approach wanted for naming shapes in geometry. For instance, according to the definition of a circle, a red circle is not different than a blue circle. Color is irrelevant to the definition of *circle*, and naming the color is subjective between the different people looking at it. Defining attributes characterize objects based on the definition of the object. Take some time and make a list of nondefining and defining attributes of the buttons. Think about more suggestions to include in figure 5.5.

Nondefining Attributes of Buttons	Defining Attributes of Buttons
Color	Shape
Shininess	Number of holes

Figure 5.5: Nondefining and defining attributes of buttons.

Although nondefining attributes may not contribute to definitions, they add to the practice of observing, examining, and describing in geometry. The latter parts of the attribute train task require you to make a train with the buttons, as shown in figure 5.6.

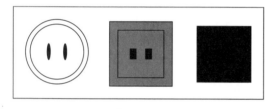

Figure 5.6: Train of buttons.

The train that you created forms a line of buttons in which the consecutive buttons share one, two, and then no attributes. For example, for the case of one attribute, perhaps the first button is white, round, and has two holes; the second button is grey, square, and has two holes; the third button is black, square, and has no holes (see figure 5.6). The first button shares only one attribute with the second button, and the second button only shares one attribute with the third button. This can be a challenging task, but these tasks help clarify what you notice about the buttons by guiding you to use your descriptions of the buttons to *analyze* and *compare* the buttons. This task helps move beyond the nondefining attribute of color and guides learners to consider other attributes to show how the buttons are alike and how they are different, as well as helping learn how to analyze and compare geometric shapes. As you work through this task with your collection of buttons, you should notice things such as the number of holes in a button and whether or not the button has a shank (the elevated part of the back of the button that holds the thread). These attributes are either present or not and help determine the type of button. Think of these attributes as defining attributes. The constraints of the task guide you to use results of your observations, examinations, and descriptions to position the buttons in the train.

Which Mathematical Practices were you engaged in while solving this task? When referring to the mathematics actions that you made during this button task, you were engaged in Mathematical Practice 1: "Make sense of problems and persevere in solving them." For each set of directions, you had to make sense of what was being asked and make decisions based on your reasoning about the buttons, such as your sorting rule. The sorting rule changed according to the directions and was, at times, challenging;

completing the task required perseverance. Mathematical Practice 6, "Attend to precision," was also evident in this task, as you had to attend to the specific detail of the buttons, particularly when you could only have no or one common attribute between consecutive buttons.

This task lends well to working in collaborative groups. As students make decisions, ask them to justify why they positioned buttons as they did. Neighboring collaborators might have some buttons in common, but they may have used them differently in the train. Hence, there might be some justifications warranted across collaborating teams as well as within a collaborating team. Ultimately, the desired outcome of the attribute train task in figure 5.4 (page 97) is to learn the difference between nondefining and defining attributes. This understanding will continue and be sharpened in the next couple of tasks. As you work through sorting activities, engagement in these practices supports your ability to reason with shapes and their attributes.

Relating Attributes of Shapes

The attribute block sorting task in figure 5.7 (page 100) makes a transition from exploring everyday objects, such as buttons, to using models of two-dimensional shapes. This transition supports a focus on defining attributes. For this example, you will use attribute blocks and two loops. If you do not already have attribute blocks, templates for them are available on **go.solution-tree.com/mathematics**; copy the blocks on colored paper, and cut them out. This model will not provide attribute blocks that are thick and thin. You can use a different material, such as foam paper, to make attribute blocks with a different thickness. For this particular task, you will not use the nondefining attributes of color, size, or thickness as sorting attributes, as these nondefining attributes do not contribute to the definitions of the two-dimensional shapes. If you do not have loops, you can just draw loops on paper.

This task begins with an open sort of attribute blocks. You have the opportunity to use observations, examinations, and descriptions to sort them. After you finish sorting, consider what defining attributes you used to create your rules. For instance, defining attributes might include shape and number of sides.

When using tasks such as this with students, at the conclusion of the open sort process, talk about the sort to introduce new geometry vocabulary in a powerful way. With attribute blocks, color might present itself as a nondefining attribute. Discussions involving defining attributes are also important here. In addition, the use of informal language like "these shapes have three lines" can include feedback such as "yes, for shapes, we call these lines *sides*." Making note of language use during and after this sorting experience provides formative assessment data regarding geometry concepts and the definitions students are developing.

Sorting loops help present information and how different parts of the information are or are not related. Essentially, the information is present in one or more parts of the sorting loops to show how the parts are related. The outcome of using the sorting loops depends on the rules used. The second part of the task—creating two rules and sorting the attribute blocks using two loops that do not overlap (disjoint loops)—provides a case where two sets of attribute blocks share no common attributes, other than that they are attribute blocks (see figure 5.8, page 100). In this case, the set of attribute blocks is described as the universal set.

This task aligns with the idea that two or more shapes can be distinct by definition and have no attributes in common, though they exist in the collection of two-dimensional shapes, as is the case with

Use a set of attribute blocks and two loops to complete the following.

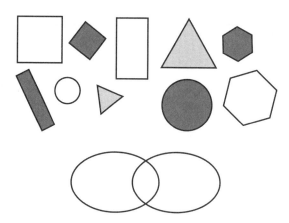

1. Sort the attribute blocks.

2. Using defining attributes, create two rules and sort the attribute blocks using two loops that do not overlap so there are blocks in each loop and there are blocks that are not in either loop.

3. Using defining attributes, create two rules and sort the attribute blocks using two intersecting loops so there are blocks in each loop that are not in the intersection of the loops, there are blocks in the intersection of the loops, and there are blocks outside of both loops.

4. Using defining attributes, create two rules and sort the attribute blocks using a loop within a loop (one inside the other) so there are blocks in the outer loop (but not in the inner loop), in the inner loop, and outside of both loops.

Figure 5.7: Attribute block sorting task.

polygons with exactly three sides and polygons with exactly four sides. Note that these rules also provide some shapes that are outside of the loops, such as circles and hexagons.

The task of creating two rules and sorting the attribute blocks using two intersected loops (creating a model of a Venn diagram) provides a case where some shapes in a set of attribute blocks have something in common with other shapes in a set of attribute blocks, but not all shapes have something in common (see figure 5.9). Hence, some blocks might be present in the intersection of the two sets while other blocks would be outside of the intersection of the two sets. For example, shapes with three or four sides could be the rule for one loop and shapes with four or more sides could be the rule for the second loop. Shapes with four sides would be in the intersection of the loops and circles would be outside both loops, but in the universe.

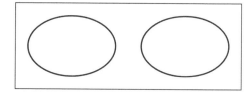

Figure 5.8: Disjoint loops.

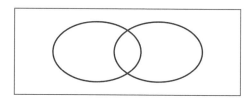

Figure 5.9: Intersected loops.

The task of creating two rules and sorting the attribute blocks using a loop within a loop provides a case where a set of attribute blocks is entirely included in another set of attribute blocks (see figure 5.10). One goal of the task in figure 5.10 is to draw attention to the relationship between squares and rectangles. If you have not considered that relationship, hold this part of the task for later. You can return to it after reading about it further on in this chapter.

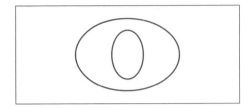

Figure 5.10: Loop within a loop.

These cases are the beginning of developing an understanding of how to *relate* shapes in geometry. How one shape relates to another shape is a large component of the content of geometry in the intermediate grades. The hands-on nature of using the sorting loops helps students explore relationships in geometry and is another context for the proper use of geometry vocabulary. As with the attribute train task (see figure 5.5, page 98), engagement in attribute block sorting (see figure 5.8) is aligned with Mathematical Practice 1, "Make sense of problems and persevere in solving them," as well as Mathematical Practice 6, "Attend to precision." Take some time to think about how you engaged in these practices while completing this task.

Sorting, Defining, and Classifying Two-Dimensional Shapes

In the next task (see figure 5.11), you will use a set of cards displaying a variety of two-dimensional shapes. We have provided these shape cards in figure 5.12. Copy them, and cut them out along the lines to form rectangular cards that contain the shapes.

1. Sort the shape cards into polygons and nonpolygons.

2. Define *polygon*.

3. Sort the simple polygons into triangles, quadrilaterals, and other polygons.

4. Name each type of triangle.

5. Classify the triangles.

6. Sort the quadrilaterals.

7. Name each type of quadrilateral.

8. Classify the quadrilaterals.

Figure 5.11: Shape cards sorting task.

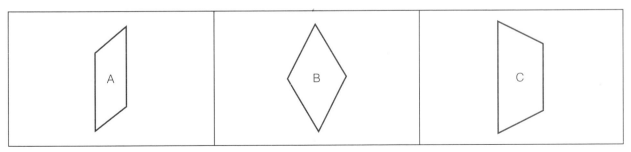

Continued ➞

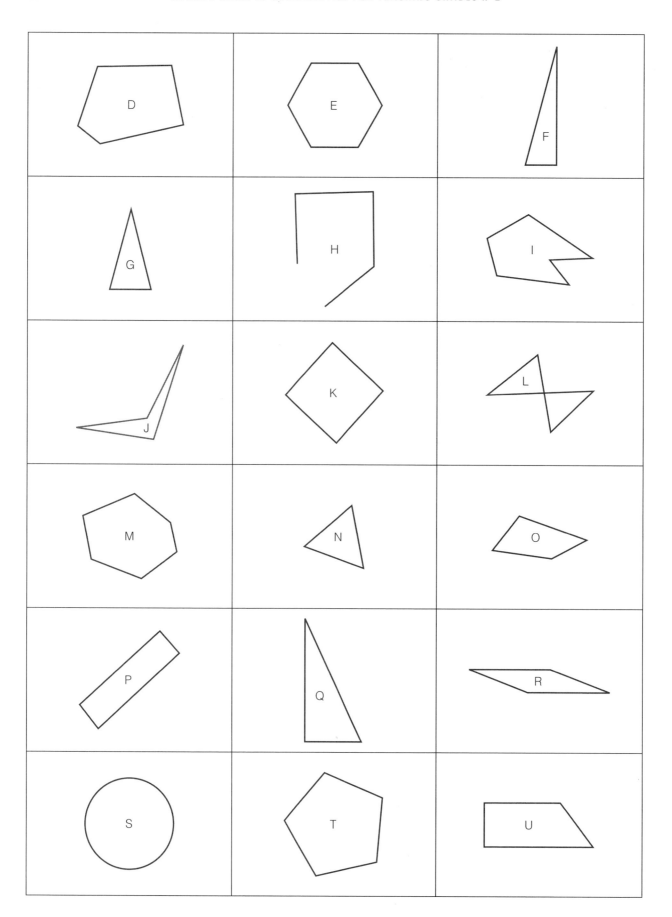

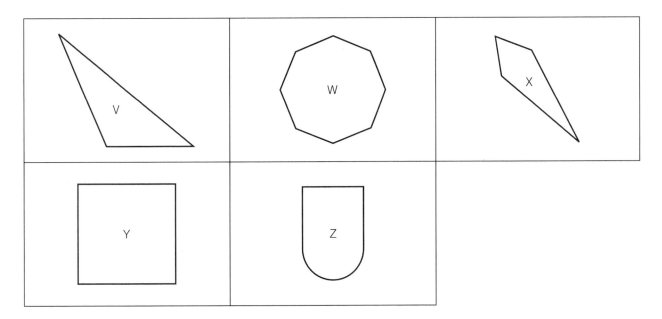

Figure 5.12: Shape cards.

*Visit **go.solution-tree.com/mathematics** for a free reproducible version of this figure.*

First, sort the shape cards into polygons and nonpolygons. To do this, consider how you define *polygon*. It is valuable for you to consider how you define various geometric shapes and how these cards align to your definitions. To refresh your understanding of the term *polygon*, it is a composition of two Greek words: *poly* and *gonia*. *Poly* means many, and *gonia* means angle or corner, so the literal meaning of the word is many angled. The number of angles also represents the number of sides in a polygon. Use this information to sort the shape cards. You might also practice *creating* examples of polygons and non-polygons of your own, as this is an important activity for studying geometry. You can create additional shapes using blank cards to include in your sort. We've provided one blank card for you in figure 5.12. If you are addressing this task within a collaborative team, you can compare the results of your sorting and discuss the validity of the shapes present in each set. This is a useful task for students as well. Observing the shapes students create and the decisions they make when sorting will provide valuable information regarding their thinking about geometry.

From this experience, try again to define *polygon*. Check your definition against this one: *A polygon is a closed two-dimensional shape made with straight line segments.* The definition you suggested might not be an exact match to this one, but any powerful mathematics definition for polygon will include that the shape is two-dimensional, that the sides must be straight (no loops, no curves), and that the shape must be closed (no openings, no gaps). Once you have a good definition for polygon, this will help situate the remaining experiences with two-dimensional shapes in the set of shape cards. Examples of nonpolygons are shapes with curved lines such as circles, half-circles, and shapes that are not closed. Which of the shape cards are nonpolygons? Cards H, S, and Z are nonpolygons. What about L? The shape on card L is actually a polygon, but it is not a *simple* polygon.

Consider the examples of simple and nonsimple polygons in table 5.1.

Table 5.1: Simple and Nonsimple Polygons

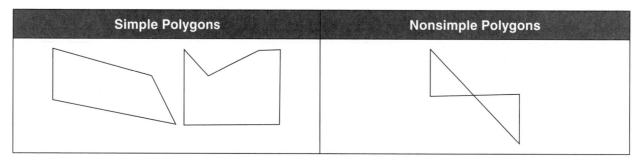

Simple Polygons	Nonsimple Polygons

Simple polygons are polygons that do not have any intersecting sides, while nonsimple polygons have intersecting sides. Simple polygons are most prevalent for K–2, but it is important to know that polygons like the nonsimple polygon provided in table 5.1 are still polygons in order to avoid creating a potential misconception—or a rule that expires—for students about what shapes are polygons.

Step 3 in this task is to sort the simple polygons into triangles, quadrilaterals, and other polygons. What are the names of the "other" polygons in the set of shape cards? How might this list of polygon names, named based on the number of sides, help you (see table 5.2)?

Table 5.2: Names of Other Polygons

Number of Sides	Name of Polygon
5	Pentagon
6	Hexagon
7	Heptagon
8	Octagon
9	Nonagon
10	Decagon

In addition, other names for polygons might use geometry vocabulary such as in table 5.3. Use this information to further describe these other polygons.

Although you might not expect K–2 students to name and define each of these polygons, students in grade 2, particularly, can use their observation, examination, and description skills to sort the polygons appropriately. You might also offer students opportunities to create, build, or draw examples of other polygons of their own.

Look again at how you sorted the cards to create a set of triangles. You should only have shapes with exactly three sides in this set. Check your sorting of quadrilaterals. You should only have shapes with four sides in this set. The remaining simple polygons should be in the third set.

Table 5.3: Categories of Polygons

Other Polygons	Definition
Regular	A polygon with all congruent sides and angles
Irregular	A polygon without all congruent sides or angles
Concave	A polygon with at least one interior angle greater than 180 degrees An alternative definition for a concave polygon is: If there exists two points inside the polygon connected by a line segment part of the line segment is outside the polygon, then the polygon is concave. For example,
Convex	A polygon with no interior angles greater than 180 degrees

Now reconsider the set of triangles, and this time, name each triangle. Naming shapes is an important component of studying geometry. You may begin with informal names and build to more formal descriptions, but it is important to model the use of formal geometry shape names.

There are two ways to name a triangle: by its angles or by the length of its sides. See tables 5.4 (page 106) and 5.5 (page 106) for the naming of triangles. Again, you might practice creating examples of triangles on your own.

Table 5.4: Triangles Named by Sides

Triangle Name	Length of Sides	Shape Cards
Equilateral triangle	All sides have the same length.	N
Isosceles triangle	At least two sides have the same length.	G, N
Scalene triangle	No sides have the same length.	F, Q, V

Table 5.5: Triangles Named by Angles

Triangle Name	Size of Angles	Shape Cards
Right triangle	One angle is a right angle.	F, Q
Acute triangle	All angles are less than 90 degrees.	G, N
Obtuse triangle	One angle is greater than 90 degrees.	V

You may notice that notations regarding the length of the sides or the size of the angles may not be present. For example, congruent sides and right angles are not indicated. As students move beyond elementary school, these designations will be necessary to demonstrate that the shapes are what they are named. Recall that considering relationships between shapes is an important component of two-dimensional geometry. Consider the six names of triangles provided in tables 5.4 and 5.5. Note that each triangle has angles and sides. With that notion in mind, which combination of triangles is possible? Use your knowledge of the six triangles to classify them by completing the chart in figure 5.13. The first two rows have been completed to help you get started.

How did you use triangle definitions in the process of classifying the triangles? You might have had difficulty if you focused on nondefining attributes rather than exclusively those attributes that define the different types of triangles. See a completed Classification of Triangles Chart in appendix A (page 139).

	Is always . . .	Is sometimes . . .	Is never . . .
An equilateral triangle	isosceles, acute		scalene, right, obtuse
An isosceles triangle		equilateral, right, acute, obtuse	scalene
A scalene triangle			
A right triangle			
An acute triangle			
An obtuse triangle			

Figure 5.13: Classification of triangles chart.

Refer to your sorting of quadrilaterals. Common quadrilaterals present in K–2 geometry are rectangles, squares, parallelograms, rhombuses (also called rhombi), and trapezoids. How do you know each is a quadrilateral? The first consideration is to check that the figure has four sides. Next, name each quadrilateral. Try to define these quadrilaterals before proceeding. Then, check your definitions with those provided in table 5.6. Be sure to avoid defining a rectangle as a quadrilateral with two short sides and two long sides. These are attributes of some rectangles, but they are not *defining* attributes of rectangles. That description limits the class of rectangles to exclude squares.

Table 5.6: Definitions of Common Quadrilaterals

Quadrilateral	Definition	Shape Cards
Parallelogram	A quadrilateral with opposite sides parallel	A, B, K, P, R, Y

Continued →

Rectangle	A quadrilateral with four right angles 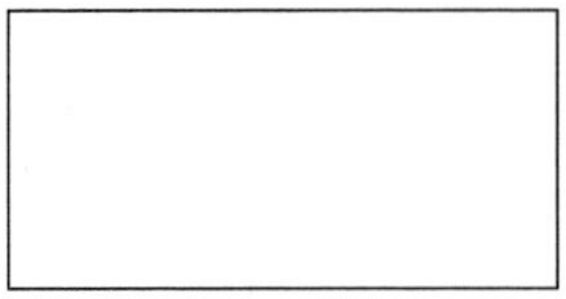	K, P, Y
Rhombus	A quadrilateral with all sides the same length 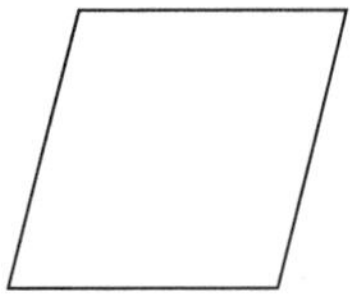	B, K, Y
Square	A quadrilateral with four right angles and all sides the same length	K, Y
Trapezoid	A quadrilateral with exactly one pair of parallel sides 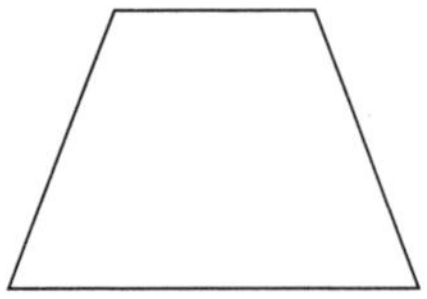	C, U
Kite	A quadrilateral with exactly two pairs of distinct congruent, adjacent sides 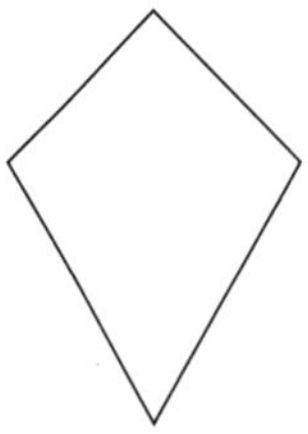	X

Consider other possible relationships among these six types of quadrilaterals. What is the relationship between kites, parallelograms, rectangles, rhombuses, squares, and trapezoids? The relationship can be shown visually. Classify these quadrilaterals using the classifying diagram in figure 5.14 by placing the name of each of the six quadrilaterals on exactly one blank in the diagram.

How did you do? A key understanding in completing this diagram is knowing that rectangles, squares, and rhombuses are all parallelograms. Of these parallelograms, there is a common trait. How can you use this knowledge to complete the task in figure 5.10 (page 101) using attribute blocks if you were unable to complete it earlier? We've provided a completed Diagram for Classifying Quadrilaterals in appendix B (page 141).

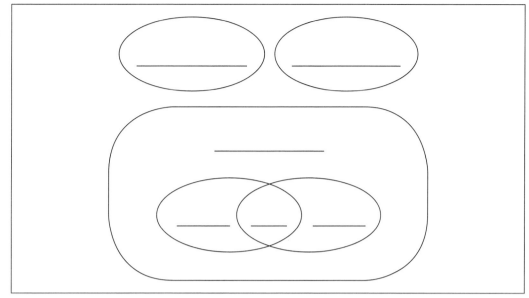

Figure 5.14: Diagram for classifying quadrilaterals.

Throughout the shape cards sorting task (see figure 5.11, page 101), you were engaged in Mathematical Practices that are similar to those used in the attribute train and block sorting tasks (see figure 5.4, page 97, and figure 5.7, page 100). The Mathematical Practice that stands out in this task is Mathematical Practice 6, "Attend to precision." When working with geometry concepts, it is important for teachers to attend to the appropriate use of geometry vocabulary, definitions, and tools to ensure that students do not acquire misconceptions during instruction.

Now use a different manipulative to create two-dimensional shapes. The task in figure 5.15 uses pattern blocks. If you do not have access to a set of pattern blocks, you can make one from colored card stock or construction paper. Before proceeding, complete the pattern blocks task in figure 5.15.

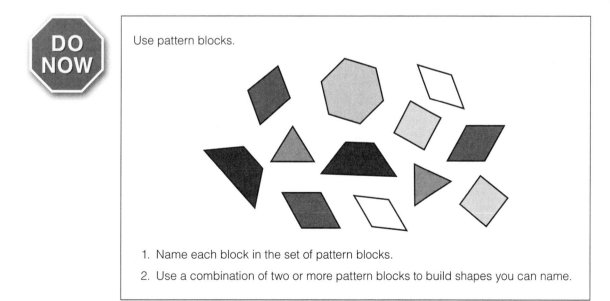

Use pattern blocks.

1. Name each block in the set of pattern blocks.
2. Use a combination of two or more pattern blocks to build shapes you can name.

Figure 5.15: Pattern blocks task.

The first part of this task is to name each block in the set of pattern blocks. This should be a review of two-dimensional shapes. The pattern block pieces in a traditional set are made of the following shapes: triangle, square, rhombus, hexagon, and trapezoid. Now, use a combination of two or more pattern blocks to build shapes you can name. Perhaps you used two equilateral triangles to build a rhombus or you used two trapezoids to build a hexagon or a parallelogram. If you did not compose those shapes, try to do so now. Composing (and decomposing) shapes is an important activity in geometry. Composing shapes is the act of taking two or more shapes to create another, larger shape, and decomposing shapes is separating a shape into two or more smaller shapes (both two-dimensional and three-dimensional shapes can be composed and decomposed). By composing and subsequently decomposing shapes, students apply their understanding of attributes and definitions of the individual shapes and newly composed shapes. Draw sketches of the shapes you composed using the pattern blocks. Consider other manipulatives that might be useful for exploring the composition of shapes in geometry. Tasks similar to this one reinforce students' abilities to reason with shapes and their attributes.

Being able to reason with shapes and their attributes is an important skill for kindergarten to grade 2 students, though not to the same degree as the tasks you have just completed. Students in K–2 need to be able to describe, identify, and compare basic shapes and their attributes. They need to be able to recognize shapes in different orientations as being the same and to experience shapes in many different configurations and understand that the shape is the same. The benefit provided by the tasks in this chapter is to use the language of geometry with your students in order to ensure that your instruction will not expire. You and your students will build a strong foundation on which later instruction will build.

Recognizing Three-Dimensional Shapes

For this section, you will need to think about the following three-dimensional solids: spheres, cubes, right rectangular prisms, right circular cones, and right circular cylinders. You can acquire models of these solids by using some everyday objects. For instance, a ball is a model for a sphere, and a cereal box is a model for a right rectangular prism. A water cooler cup is a model for a right circular cone, and a can is a model for a right circular cylinder. Make a list of other everyday objects that can serve as models for three-dimensional shapes.

In a practical sense, two-dimensional shapes are modeled as drawings or shapes on a plane, a two-dimensional surface. Because these shapes are two-dimensional (having only length and width), they have no depth or thickness. This can be confusing when using a three-dimensional model to represent a two-dimensional shape, such as a triangle cut out of construction paper (which really does have some thickness). In theory, one can't cut out or hold a triangle, because in concept, it only has two dimensions, but you need to create cutouts and shapes as a way to make the content accessible to learners. Three-dimensional shapes are modeled as solids in three dimensions as they have length, width, and height. Consider that a rectangular prism is composed of six rectangles and a cylinder is composed of two circles and a wrapped rectangle. With a mixed pile of shapes, students should be able to distinguish between the two-dimensional shapes and the three-dimensional shapes.

Now sort the shapes you have collected as described in figure 5.16.

Use a set of two- and three-dimensional shapes.

1. Distinguish two-dimensional shapes from three-dimensional shapes.
2. Sort the three-dimensional shapes.
3. Describe defining attributes of the three-dimensional shapes.
4. Name the three-dimensional shapes.

Figure 5.16: Two- and three-dimensional shapes task.

Did you sort the three-dimensional shapes according to the polygons that compose them? K–2 students might begin with an informal approach to sorting the three-dimensional shapes. For instance, they might sort the shapes into two groups, one group of three-dimensional shapes that can roll (spheres, cylinders, cones) and one group of three-dimensional shapes that cannot roll across a table (cubes, prisms). Instruction in grades 3–5 builds on that foundation. What sorting groups did you create? Perhaps you sorted by which shapes have flat sides and which do not or which shapes have only polygonal faces and which do not. Consider your observations and descriptions of each three-dimensional shape and make a list of the defining attributes of each shape. This is started for you in table 5.7.

Table 5.7: Attributes of Common Three-Dimensional Solids

Three-Dimensional Shapes	Example of a Defining Attribute
Sphere	No flat faces
Cube	Six faces
Right rectangular prism	Rectangular faces
Right circular cone	Only one base
Right circular cylinder	Two circular bases

As you work with these three-dimensional shapes, practice using their proper names and drawing each of them. Consider how you will support your students to begin to develop the correct language and understandings of the relationships between these shapes. Students in the K–2 grade band need to be able to distinguish between two-dimensional shapes (such as rectangles, squares, trapezoids, triangles, and circles) and three-dimensional shapes (such as cubes, right rectangular prisms, right circular cones, and right circular cylinders) and use them to compose and decompose composite shapes.

The Classroom

Now that you have explored your own thinking about plane and solid geometry concepts, turn your attention to explore what this will look like in the classroom. The included video links provide important insight into student thinking about geometry. How do the students consider different attributes of the shapes they are given? How does the teacher guide the lesson? Take the time to watch the following video in its entirety.

www.solution-tree.com/Comparing_Plane_Shapes

Now that you have had the opportunity to view young students compare attributes of two-dimensional shapes, what is your perspective about the progression of geometry? In this video, the teacher first narrows the discussion of shapes to two shapes: a circle and a rectangle. The goal of the lesson is to build students' skills of observation, description, and comparison of shapes. These skills serve as a foundation in geometry and carry across plane and solid geometry. They also give students context for Mathematical Practice 3, "Construct viable arguments and critique the reasoning of others."

Initially, the students' observations focus on the attribute of color. This is an acceptable anchor to include for younger learners. However, if you desire to avoid students focusing on the attribute of color as a difference between multiple shapes, simply present shapes of the same color to eliminate that difference. With further prompting, a student moves beyond color and describes the number of sides of the rectangle, and another student describes the circle as having only curves and no vertices. These descriptions include terminology that some young students might not have, but it is important to help students build formal mathematics terminology and to do so according to Mathematical Practice 6, "Attend to precision," because it is just as important to be precise with mathematical terminology as it is with mathematical computation. As the video continues, you will notice that another student has even more advanced geometry vocabulary when she states that the rectangle is "two-dimensional because it lays flat." Note that the strategy of thinking about a shape being two-dimensional because it lays flat in a book is an informal way of characterizing two-dimensional shapes, not a way of defining two-dimensional shapes.

The teacher selects two more shapes for students to discuss: a triangle and a rectangle. In this section of the video, students again focus on the number of sides and the number of vertices. However, another student connects his understanding of the triangle to a real-life object (pizza); this strategy can be very helpful for students' developing understanding of shapes. To further the exploration of shapes, using the combination of *alike* and *different* helps students advance their mathematical language and their understanding of the shapes. The final comparison between a rectangle and circle provides an opportunity for students to distinguish shapes that have straight sides and shapes that do not have straight sides. It is important to note that the teacher's questions and the students' exploration of the shapes drive the learning experience. Furthermore, by using a limited number of shapes, the teacher is able to target students' focus better than if each student had many shapes to observe, describe, and compare.

The first video demonstrates the important foundational work that students need to learn for categorizing geometry shapes: observation, description, and comparison. In the second video, a teacher asks grade 3 students to make a square and a rectangle. How does the teacher facilitate the discussion? Watch the video in its entirety before proceeding.

www.solution-tree.com/Defining_and
_Classifying_Squares_and_Rectangles

Now that you have had the opportunity to watch students actively engage in developing understanding of squares and rectangles, what are your thoughts? Consider the focus of the lesson. Think about the exploratory nature of it, and note the tools provided to the students and how they are used. What kinds of questions are posed? How do students demonstrate their learning?

Perhaps after viewing the entire video, you notice that the focus of the lesson is not revealed in the teacher's introduction or in the first instruction the teacher gives. However, these two items provide an important foundation for the lesson. The introduction offers the students an opportunity to explore quadrilaterals, and the first instruction of using the available manipulative to make a square engages each student to recall how to use the manipulative and how to form the model for a square. During this event, the teacher quickly observes how students are interacting with the manipulative to create the model. When noticing that most students have completed the task, the teacher asks the students to hold up what they've made. What is really important at this point is that the teacher does not indicate who is or who isn't holding up a square. The teacher invites the students to make the assessment by asking, "What do you see?" This gives students ownership in the lesson. You will note that the students respond in unison that all of the shapes held up are squares. It is at this point that the teacher indicates that she sees one shape being held up that is not a square. Again, she poses to the class the task of determining where the nonsquare is rather than simply pointing out the nonsquare and taking ownership away from the students. With the prompting to further observe the shapes being held up, a student responds that he thinks he sees the shape that is not a square. He explains his thinking, and the teacher gives a second student an opportunity to respond to the first student's conclusion. This exchange supports Mathematical Practice 3, "Construct viable arguments and critique the reasoning of others." In the safety of the learning environment, the student is willing to confront the inaccurate model for a square and to state his position clearly. However, the teacher's further questioning of the student who does not build the accurate model for a square leads to the student using the manipulative to make better sense of her understanding of a square. This teaching moment also represents the powerful impact that the right choice of manipulative can have on students' learning.

The next experience in this video is the teacher challenging the students to make a rectangle. Subsequently, the teacher asks the students to hold up their rectangles. The teacher is operating on an assumption that students will most likely make the traditional rectangle with two long sides and two short sides. In preparation for this assumption, the teacher decides to introduce students to a different perspective of the rectangle by using the strategy of "I saw someone . . .". By engaging students with a possible response from another student, the teacher can introduce a concept without causing alarm. Here the teacher says that she saw someone hold up a square in response to the request to make a rectangle. This is a critical point in the lesson because it is the marker for students developing an understanding of the relationship between squares and rectangles. The teacher then provides an opportunity for the students to engage in discourse about this new perspective. You can observe some students in the video making the declaration that "a square is a rectangle," but the strength of this statement is not evident from mere observation. Clearly, the teacher recognizes the need to further question students' understanding of the relationship between squares and rectangles.

The teacher asks students to share their thinking, and through the dialogue that follows, the students' understandings and misunderstandings are revealed. For instance, a student responds by saying, "A rectangle doesn't have all equal sides; it has two short sides and two long sides." This perspective is not surprising and is often the result of limited exposure to developing the appropriate definition of rectangle and limited exposure to models of rectangle that reflect this definition. This begs attention to Mathematical Practice 6, "Attend to precision," during instruction in mathematics. A quadrilateral with four sides (and four right angles)—two long sides and two short sides—is an example of a rectangle but not the definition of rectangle. Again, the teacher asks who agrees with this statement. Upon seeing that the majority of students do agree, she confronts the students with the cognitive challenge that what the previous student said is indeed not correct. After allowing for additional discussion, she asks, "Where are you now?"

One student in the class, who states that he is speaking for himself as well as his group, shares results of comparing squares to rectangles—they both have four right angles and they both have opposite sides equal. With the teacher's prompting, the student is able to conclude that a square is a rectangle, but one with all equal sides. However, note that the discourse does not end with this declaration because the teacher needs more certainty that other students have also advanced their understanding of the relationship between squares and rectangles. She engages the class by asking, "What did he say?" This is an excellent strategy for assessing students' clarification about what their peers have said and also provides students an opportunity to support or refute what they've heard another student say. In addition, the teacher uses all three layers of facilitation throughout the lesson—facilitating engagement of the whole class, small groups, and individual students.

Finally, the teacher challenges the students to make a square that is not a rectangle, and the students determine that this cannot be done because a square is also a rectangle. At the conclusion of this lesson, you may wonder what other instructional moves the teacher could have made to encourage discourse and scaffold students to understand the relationship between a square and a rectangle. Note that this primary goal of the lesson was not presented in a straightforward fashion because simply telling students the relationship does not support their understanding of the relationship. Giving students an opportunity to explore the relationship is the best course of action.

TQE Process

At this point, it may be helpful to watch the second video again (page 113). Pay close attention to the tasks, questioning, and opportunities to collect evidence of student learning.

The TQE process can help you frame your observations. Teachers who have a deep understanding of the mathematics they teach:

- Select appropriate *tasks* to support identified learning goals

- Facilitate productive *questioning* during instruction to engage students in the Mathematical Practices

- Collect and use student *evidence* in the formative assessment process during instruction

This lesson's *task* focuses on classifying squares and rectangles, though this is not apparent at the beginning of the lesson. The goal of the lesson is originally presented as exploring quadrilaterals. This task is designed with the expectation that many students will define rectangles as having two long sides and two short sides, excluding the possibility of a square being a rectangle. The sequence of the activities in this task highlights this common misconception; the learning outcome is for students to know that all squares are also rectangles. If the learning goal of this task had been presented at the beginning of the lesson, the dissonance of the lesson would be lost. Thus, it is important to consider how to present the learning goal in the design of the task when the plan is for students to discover a new relationship (or correct a commonly held misconception). Note also how the choice of manipulative (AngLegs) to model the shapes supports the teacher being able to see how the students are constructing the shapes, as the sides of the same length are the same color. This allows the teacher to quickly determine which students have constructed squares and which students have constructed rectangles that are not squares.

Notice how the teacher's *questioning* guides the student's role throughout the lesson. With the "What do you see?" and "What did he say?" type of questions, the students appear to be in charge of the lesson. However, the teacher is, in fact, guiding the lesson by asking the right questions and selecting the student responses that will move the class toward achieving the learning goal. She uses questioning to create a climate in which students are leading the sense making and their strategies are guiding the work of the class. This climate is supported through questioning, appropriate use of student work, and the "I saw someone . . ." strategy. This strategy, when the teacher says she's seen another student take a certain action, is beneficial for students to think that other students advance the thinking that moves the class forward. It is important to consider and plan what examples or models will be helpful to present to students as a hypothetical situation to advance their learning. By asking other questions, such as "Where are you now?" and "What did he say?," the teacher is engaging students and encouraging discussion.

The teacher is able to collect *evidence* of student learning during the lesson. The choice of manipulative makes the recognition of who can accurately construct a square or a rectangle easy, and having the students display and analyze their squares leads to an example of Mathematical Practice 6, "Attend to precision." Clearly, the students have developed the norm of taking a risk to show their work in the class. This is important to note because the formative assessment process can support assessment of multiple students at one time, not just an occurrence between the teacher and a single student. The teacher also collects information on how students define rectangles, first by allowing them to construct them, and then, after seeing their constructions, by asking who agrees that a rectangle must have two short sides and two long sides. In seeing that all students agree with that definition, the teacher tells them that this is incorrect. With her prompting and some exploration, the class is able to conclude that a square is a rectangle, but one with all sides equal. Note that the discourse does not end with this statement, as the teacher needs more evidence that other students have advanced their understanding of the relationship between squares and rectangles.

An additional consideration is how to recognize and respond to student errors. In the next section, you will review geometry topics as they relate to common errors of students. This will provide another plan of action as you learn to address misconceptions by recognizing their source and thinking about ways to assist students.

The Response

Commonly expected difficulties in K–2 involve the language and related representations of geometry. Students may confuse the vocabulary because there are simply so many new terms present in geometry. It will help to use strategies such as a mathematics journal, a word wall, a classroom dictionary, and lots of discourse to support the appropriate use of geometry vocabulary. Each of these and other instructional strategies should include the pairing of geometry terms and pictorial or concrete representations. You should deliberately use more than just the common ways of representing shapes, such as triangles with a horizontal line segment at the bottom of the drawing, as students need to accurately produce and identify a variety of representations.

Another frequent difficulty is with the definition of geometrical terms that appear to be correct but, in fact, only help students develop misconceptions. For example, when a rectangle is defined as a four-sided shape with two long sides and two short sides, this excludes the square as a rectangle, when in fact a square is a special case of a rectangle. Hence, an appropriate definition for *rectangle* is a four-sided shape (quadrilateral) with four right angles. The length of sides is not relevant to the definition of rectangle. However, if a rectangle has all sides of equal length, this type of rectangle is a square.

The next example deals with the language of *at least* and *exactly*. Each phrase brings a different perspective to a definition. While *at least* opens up a definition, *exactly* narrows the definition. For instance, consider the two possible definitions for an isosceles triangle.

1. An isosceles triangle is a triangle with at least two sides the same length.

2. An isosceles triangle is a triangle with exactly two sides the same length.

The first definition opens up the possibility for equilateral triangles, triangles with all sides the same length, to also be isosceles triangles. However, the second definition would not include equilateral triangles. While both definitions are acceptable, the first, less restrictive definition is the one we have adopted in this book.

Consider these two accepted definitions for the trapezoid.

1. A trapezoid is a quadrilateral with one pair of parallel sides.

2. A trapezoid is a quadrilateral with exactly one pair of parallel sides.

The first definition opens up the possibility for parallelograms, rectangles, squares, and rhombuses to be trapezoids. However, the second definition would not accommodate quadrilaterals with more than one pair of parallel sides. In this case, the second more restrictive definition is aligned with our views and is used in this book. What this means in general, though, is that it is important to be very clear about the supporting phrases in mathematics definitions so that students do not develop misunderstandings in geometry.

Because language is at the forefront of difficulties in geometry, students *and* teachers must engage in Mathematical Practice 6, "Attend to precision," during geometry instruction. If teachers are precise with geometry language, their students will be precise with language.

Reflections

1. What do you feel are the key points in this chapter?

2. What challenges might you face when implementing the key ideas from this chapter? How will you overcome them?

3. What are the important features for developing an understanding of geometry, and how will you ensure your instruction embeds the support needed for these features?

4. Select a recent lesson you have taught or observed focused on geometry. Relate this lesson to the TQE process.

5. What changes will you make to your planning and instruction based on what you read and considered from this chapter?

CHAPTER 6

Measurement

In kindergarten through grade 2, topics in measurement are primarily related to linear measurement, time, and money. Contexts related to measurement offer opportunities for students to engage in problem solving in real-world contexts.

The Challenge

The initial task in this chapter (see figure 6.1) provides an opportunity for you to engage in problem solving related to linear measurement, time, and money, respectively—each of the primary measurement topics in K–2. Be sure to solve each problem before proceeding. While solving the task, think about how you might use the problems, or modify the problems, with your students.

1. Sergei and Lois each measure the length of the same object. Sergei says the length is 5 units. Lois says the length is 15 units. How can they both be correct?

2. What time is it when the *hour* hand is on the 24th *minute* mark?

3. Jackie had 45 cents in her purse, but she has no dimes. What coins could she have in her purse? What process did you use to determine the coins?

Figure 6.1: Measurement problems task.

The first problem addresses concepts typically taught in grade 2 involving identifying units, selecting units, and measuring with units of different lengths. Students are quick to assume that others measured incorrectly rather than identifying that they are measuring with different units. Students benefit from experiences that provide opportunities to explore units, particularly nonstandard units that can be used to measure length, such as paper clips and toothpicks. Who had the longer unit, Sergei or Lois? Since the length of the object is given to be the same, you can see that Sergei's unit was longer because it took less iteration (repetitive use of a single unit of measurement) of that unit to measure the object than with Lois's unit. This problem provides a nice opening to ask an advancing question for students who understand this concept earlier than their peers. Advancing questions help provide enrichment to students who have already met the learning goal. You could ask, "How many of Lois's units would it take to make a unit that is the length of Sergei's?" This is a transition into using a singular, agreed-on unit of measure. This is a very challenging task for young learners and should be used with those students who will benefit from tasks that are significantly beyond their peers. A common error with the first problem is to conclude that Lois's unit is longer because her measure is greater. This addresses the inverse relationship between the length of the unit and the number of units needed to measure a given object. The application of this concept is not just for nonstandard units but also for pairings of standard units, such as inches and feet or centimeters and meters.

The second problem is quite challenging and is not appropriate for most K–2 students; it is intended to help *you* consider why telling time causes students so much confusion. However, it could be modified so that it is appropriate for grade 2. Far more can be determined from the hour hand than is typically explored. Examine the clock in figure 6.2. It does not have a minute hand, only an hour hand.

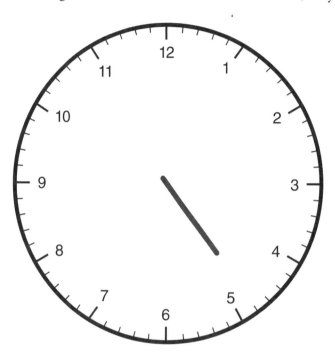

Figure 6.2: What time is it when the hour hand is pointing at the twenty-fourth minute mark?

What time do you think it is when the hour hand is on the twenty-fourth minute mark? Do you think it is 4:24? How about 4:45? Both answers are incorrect. If you said 4:24, you may be confusing the role of the hour hand with the minute hand. The hour hand is pointing at the twenty-fourth minute mark, but that does not indicate twenty-four minutes. If you said 4:45, you are not providing the time to the nearest minute.

It is 4:48 when the hour hand is on the twenty-fourth minute mark. But how is this determined? It is determined by making sense of the amount of time that elapses as the hour hand points to one minute and then the next as it makes its way around an analog clock. As the hour hand passes from the four o'clock hour to the five o'clock hour, it passes through five minute marks. Therefore, in a span of sixty minutes, twelve minutes pass every time the hour hand goes from one minute mark to the next. The twenty-fourth minute mark is four minute marks after the four. Therefore it is 4 × 12 minutes after four o'clock, or 4:48. This is the only correct answer, and it involves engaging in Mathematical Practice 7, "Look for and make use of structure."

Now that you have made sense of this problem, how might you adapt it for students in grade 2? One way would be to ask students what time it is when the hour hand is pointing halfway between the four and the five on the clock. We will discuss this approach later in this chapter.

The third problem has multiple correct answers. What is most interesting about this problem is an exploration of the strategies that determine the combinations of coins that will equal forty-five cents. Did you begin by determining the choice of coins haphazardly? Did you start by using the coins with the greatest values first (quarters and nickels), or did you start with pennies? How might your strategies differ from those students might use? What would you learn from a student who began with forty-five pennies compared to a student who started with the greatest values of coins first?

This problem could be one that students continue to work on, adding their new solutions to a bulletin board posted in the room. If this problem seems too challenging for some of your students, how might you make it more attainable? Perhaps you could include the use of dimes or only use dimes and pennies. The topic of measurement is one that has many access points for students. It is relevant to students' daily activities and extends beyond what students might encounter through everyday living outside of school.

The Progression

Measurement builds on work in geometry. In geometry, students explore and describe attributes of shapes. With measurement, attributes are narrowed to those that are measureable. Measureable attributes include, but are certainly not limited to, length and weight. After students are able to describe measureable attributes, they learn to estimate, compare, and eventually measure those attributes using standard units. A progression for learning measurement is as follows.

- Identify and describe measureable attributes.

- Compare objects using measurable attributes directly and indirectly.

- Identify and select units (nonstandard and standard).

- Estimate length.

- Measure and describe length using a whole number of length units.

- Iterate units for linear measurement.

- Explore the inverse relationship between the size of the unit and the number of units needed to complete a linear measurement process.

- Measure length using tools like rulers.

A learning progression for telling time follows.

- Tell time to the hour.

- Tell time to the half hour.

- Tell time to the nearest five minutes.

- Use a.m. and p.m. when telling time.

- Tell time to the nearest minute.

- Solve word problems involving addition and subtraction of time intervals in minutes.

Finally, a progression for understanding money builds on solving problems involving dollars, quarters, dimes, nickels, and pennies.

Here, we'll detail the progression at each grade level.

Kindergarten

In kindergarten, students describe measureable attributes. They might explore one object and discuss what is measureable about that specific object. For example, kindergarteners are able to use a book as the object and discuss what they could measure with the book. Before students proceed, they might use the book as a way of estimating what they plan to measure about a given object. For instance, consider a student who suggests she could use the book to measure the lengths of the sides of an object (such as a table), measure (compare the book to) the weight of an object, or use the color of the book to "measure" the color of an object. On that note, while color *is* an attribute, it is not a *measureable* attribute, and students will develop this notion by considering their differing opinions about the color of an object.

Once students are able to identify measureable attributes, they compare two objects that have a measureable attribute in common. For example, a student could compare his mathematics book to his reading book to first estimate and then determine which book is heavier or "taller." He does this by holding an object in each hand to determine which book feels heavier and by standing one book up against the other to see which is taller. This direct comparison process works best with objects that young learners can actually hold in their hands or place together to support the students' observations about the objects.

Grade 1

In grade 1, students move from comparing two objects directly to ordering three objects using indirect measurement techniques. The students might estimate and then compare their reading book to their mathematics book and see that their mathematics book is taller. Then, they estimate and compare their reading book to their journal and see that their journal is shorter than their reading book. Since their mathematics book is taller than their reading book and their journal is shorter than their reading book, they know that the order of books from tallest to shortest is their mathematics book, their reading book, and then their journal. Thus, the students compare the mathematics book and the journal indirectly by using the reading book. A goal is for students to see this technique as helpful when comparing two objects that cannot be measured directly easily—for example, comparing the heights of their teacher's desk to the principal's desk. Since the desks are difficult to move, the students could use a nonstandard unit, like a length of string, to compare to each of the desks. If the teacher's desk is the same height as the length of string and the principal's desk is taller than the length of string, the students conclude that the principal's desk is taller than their teacher's desk through indirect measurement.

Indirect measurement leads to the use of units to measure. The focus in grade 1 is on estimating, using nonstandard and, subsequently, standard units to measure length. Students use iterations of a unit shorter than what they want to measure by laying copies of the unit end to end with no gaps or overlaps, counting the number of units needed, and then reporting that number and the unit name to complete the measurement process.

Time is first introduced as a measure in grade 1. Students measure time to the hour and half hour. They tell and write time using both analog and digital clocks.

Grade 2

In grade 2, concepts and skills related to estimation and both linear and time measurement are extended and money is introduced. Linear measurement is extended with the introduction of tools such as rulers and meter sticks. Students focus on the unit of measure by measuring the same object with units of different length and determining that the longer the unit, the smaller quantity of the unit it takes to measure an object. This exploration helps students provide reasonable estimates of lengths given units in inches, feet, centimeters, and meters. Eventually, students are able to solve real-world problems involving addition and subtraction and comparison involving length.

Also in grade 2, students tell time to the nearest five minutes and use a.m. and p.m. It is most helpful for students to connect their learning of time with real-life activities, specifically so that students have contexts for understanding a.m. and p.m.

Students also solve word problems comprising money amounts, specifically dollar bills, quarters, dimes, nickels, and pennies. Just as in grade 1 with time, grade 2 is the first point at which money is introduced as a measure. Students explore and record money amounts using the $ and ¢ symbols appropriately.

The Mathematics

Measurement provides a rich context to explore reasoning and sense making. The more experiences you have conjecturing about measurements and then testing those conjectures, the better you will become at estimating measures. The same is true for your students. Students in K–2 will need to be able to make sense of linear measurement, time, and money.

Making Sense of Linear Measurement

Linear measurement transitions from comparing directly by placing one object alongside another to see which is longer or taller to comparing indirectly by using an intermediary object like a length of string to compare two objects. Eventually, indirect measurement leads to measuring with units. The lengths of two objects can be sorted by comparing the number of units that measure each object.

Students begin to use units to measure length by iterating these units. For example, a student might use square color tiles by laying them edge to edge in order to see how many color tiles it takes to measure the width of her desk. The student then counts each tile to determine the width of the desk in tiles. Measuring using units like tiles is eventually replaced with using inches and other standard units of measure. The transition from iterating objects and counting the number of objects to measuring with rulers is a difficult one for students. Part of this difficulty stems from how the unit is counted. Consider figure 6.3. What might cause students difficulty? How is the concept of using iterations of units to measure different from using a ruler?

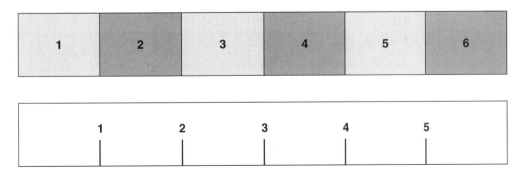

Figure 6.3: Measuring with tiles or a ruler.

Think about the process students use to measure with color tiles. They line up the tiles and then count them. They likely place their finger on the center of each tile and count the tiles one by one. Now consider how to use the ruler to measure the same object to the nearest unit. The "zero" point of the ruler is lined up with one end of the object, and the length is determined by identifying the end of the unit that most closely matches the end of the object. The units are counted at the end of each unit rather than in the center. Some teachers find it difficult to distinguish between these differences, but transitioning from counting units to using a ruler often feels monumental to students. Addressing these differences explicitly with students as the ruler is introduced might help avoid some of the errors experienced, such as using the midpoint between the tick marks on the ruler as the inch mark or counting *every* tick mark on the ruler—including the mark at zero—to determine the length of an object. Understanding these misconceptions helps provide support for students to overcome them.

Regardless of the tool, students should use estimates of lengths along with their measures as a means of determining if their measurements are reasonable. Students might conjecture regarding the length of an object prior to measuring it and then measure it to see how their estimate compares. It is also useful for students to have benchmarks to use when determining their estimates. For example, if a student knows that the desk is twenty-six inches tall, he might use that to make a guess that the seat of a chair is fifteen inches tall. Making a list of common items and then measuring their lengths to use as benchmarks is a useful technique for making estimates of other objects.

How are you at estimating lengths? What benchmarks do you use? The task in figure 6.4 provides a list of common classroom items. Estimate the length of each object and then measure them to see how close your estimates are to the actual measures.

Item	Estimated Length	Actual Length
Height of the teacher's desk		
Width of the classroom door		
Length of the bulletin board		
Length of a new pencil		

Figure 6.4: Conjectures for lengths of everyday classroom items task.

Were your estimates close? How did you determine if they were close enough? This idea lends itself to engaging in Mathematical Practice 6, "Attend to precision." Determining what is close enough provides the basis for rich discussions with students.

Linear measurement opens the door to many other applications of measurement in later grades. For example, students can add linear measurements of each side of a simple polygon (squares, rectangles) to find the perimeter of the polygon. Students can multiply the "length" linear measure and the "width" linear measure of select simple polygons to find the area of those polygons. However, the formula for area, while supported by the exploration of measurement in K–2, is best addressed by describing area as equal size pieces (square units) that cover a whole. This exploration of area provides valuable opportunities for exploring flexible thinking and visualization as well as for linking measurement to geometry and later work with fractions. Consider the challenge provided in the geoboard fourths task in figure 6.5. It calls for the use of a geoboard, but if one is not available to you, the activity can be completed using virtual geoboard manipulatives or on geoboard dot paper, as in the figure. The goal is to make fourths in as many different ways as you can. If the size of the whole remains constant, what could *different* mean? Think about this and attempt the task before reading further.

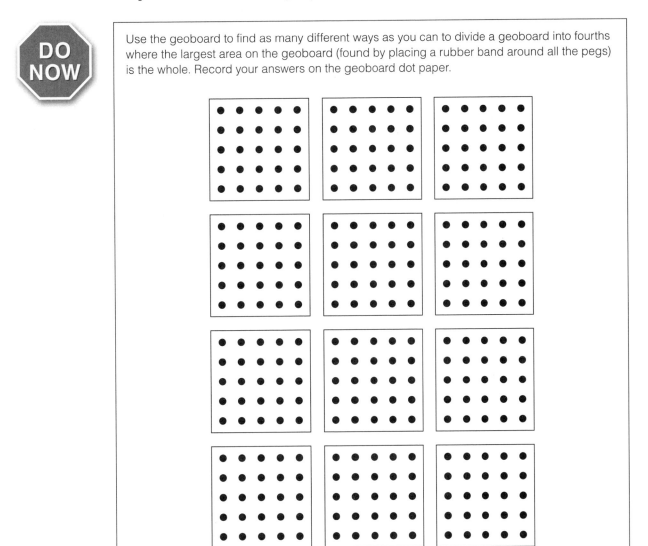

Use the geoboard to find as many different ways as you can to divide a geoboard into fourths where the largest area on the geoboard (found by placing a rubber band around all the pegs) is the whole. Record your answers on the geoboard dot paper.

Figure 6.5: Geoboard fourths task.

*Visit **go.solution-tree.com/mathematics** for a free reproducible version of this figure.*

It is likely that you began this task rather quickly, creating then drawing representations of fourths provided in figure 6.6 (page 126). However, once you drew these fourths, were you at a loss? Perhaps you started to draw a rotation of the first illustration in figure 6.6, but then determined that this representation was not truly different because it was a rotation of the original image.

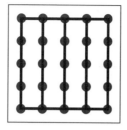 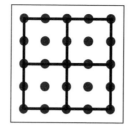 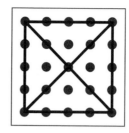

Figure 6.6: Examples of geoboard fourths.

It takes a shift in perspective to continue with this task. That shift is one that is addressed in grade 2 when students realize that equal shares do not require congruent shapes. The parts do not need to be the same *shape* to be fourths. They only need to be the same *size*. Consider the options provided in figure 6.7. Two of the illustrations are correct but one is not. Which ones represent fourths, and which one does not?

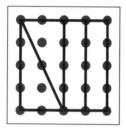 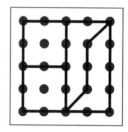 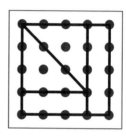

Figure 6.7: Two examples and one non-example of geoboard fourths.

One way to ensure that the geoboard is divided into four equal parts is to determine the area of the geoboard and then see if each smaller area represents one-fourth of the total area. The total area can be described as being sixteen square units. This can be determined by counting the squares made by four pegs that form the vertices of the smallest square on a geoboard. After you determine the total area of the geoboard, you know that each fourth, while not necessarily the same shape, must be four square units in area. You can see that the first illustration has two rectangles: each with an area of four square units; and a larger rectangle divided into two congruent triangles. That rectangle that is divided into two triangles is half the area of the geoboard so it is eight square units. This makes the triangles each four square units. Since each of the four sections is the same size, together, they represent fourths of the geoboard.

While the second illustration is quite unusual, it also represents fourths. This can be determined using logic similar to that used to make sense of the first illustration. The third illustration is not fourths. The rectangle along the bottom of the geoboard is only three square units, which means that the sections are not all in equal-size parts. Thus, the illustration cannot represent fourths.

This task provides an opportunity to extend exploration of measurement to measuring area. It is directly related to experiences in grade 3 where students are asked to find areas by counting square units. It is appropriate as a challenge in grade 2 as students explore the idea that equal shares do not require parts that are the same shape. This task can be part of an ongoing challenge using a bulletin board where students add their own geoboard fourths to the display, as long as their fourths are different from those already on the board. Checking to ensure that their contributions are unique helps students see area in ways that will help them in later grades.

Making Sense of Telling Time

The concept of time is abstract and can be challenging for young learners. Its application in life can be even more abstract, especially in contexts where learners may have little exposure to telling time and determining elapsed time as important components of their daily lives. For instance, in some home contexts, the family schedule of who is doing what and when is reviewed each day, exposing young learners to the application of time in real life. Students who enter school without this early advantage of exposure to the application of time will find learning time concepts challenging in the school setting.

Seeing the clock is also quite challenging. You are likely accustomed to seeing an analog clock and telling time without much cognitive load. This is not the case for young learners. When students begin the process of learning to tell time on an analog clock, there is much for them to see and decode. You might have experienced this with the challenge question regarding time in figure 6.1 (page 119). Take a close look at the clock provided in figure 6.8. Try to identify aspects of the clock that might cause students confusion.

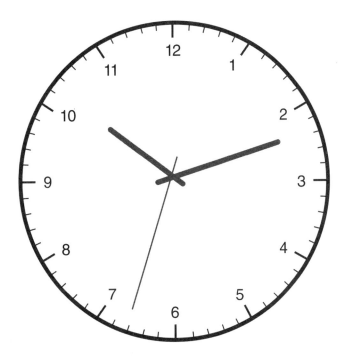

Figure 6.8: Making sense of the analog clock.

Did you notice the order of the numbers seems to change from one side of the clock to the other? On the right side, the numbers go from lesser to greater as you scan from the top of the clock to the bottom, while on the left side they go from greater to lesser as you scan from the top to the bottom. Additionally, if you begin at 1, you can count as you were taught until you get to 12; and then you suddenly start over again as you continue around the circle. Moreover, there are the sticks that go around in circles. They are called "hands," but they really don't look like (human) hands in the way young learners might expect.

One hand identifies the hour, another the minutes, and still another the seconds. Why does the shortest hand identify the longest unit of time and the longest hand identify the shortest unit of time? How can the number 3 on the clock signify three o'clock, a quarter of an hour, fifteen minutes, and fifteen seconds all at once? The clock is quite confusing when viewed in this light. One way to reduce the complexity of the clock is to temporarily remove some of the extraneous information it contains. Just using the hour hand and arranging the clock into a number line helps (see figure 6.9).

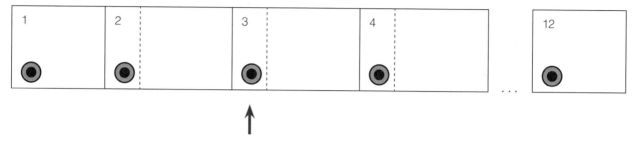

Figure 6.9: A one-handed clock number line with the hour hand pointing at three o'clock.

This model can be introduced in kindergarten without the reference to time. They can use the model to discuss number sequence as well as position words, such as *between, before, after,* and so on. Then, in grade 1, the model can be introduced as a version of a linear clock. With this version of the clock, students in grade 1 can determine the hour and half hour just by focusing on the hour hand. They can see in figure 6.9 that the hour hand is pointing at the 3 so it is three o'clock. You can create this tool using twelve index cards and connecting them with brads. This allows students to see a linear model of the circular clock.

Students can indicate the location of the hour hand to show half past four o'clock by positioning the hour hand at the midpoint between the 4 and the 5, and so on. Once students are comfortable reading and indicating time to the hour and half hour using the clock number line, the index cards can be connected at the twelve and one to make a loop, more closely representing an analog clock face. Eventually, students should transition to using an analog clock with a minute hand, but continue to remind them of the importance of the hour hand as they use the minute hand to tell time more precisely.

The introduction of the minute hand involves applying work with number and skip counting. Think about how to determine the time when the hour hand is slightly after the three and the minute hand is on the three. Students who do not know the time automatically may count by fives three times to determine the number of minutes. They say, "Five, ten, fifteen" as they look at the 1, 2, and 3 on the clock face to determine that the time is 3:15. Students also use skip counting when determining money amounts made up of coins. However, skip counting with money is more complicated, as the multiple is not always five; it depends on the values of the coins.

Making Sense of Money

The presence of money in many contexts in life would lead one to think that it should be quite easy for young learners to learn money concepts. However, while some students have early exposure to applications of money concepts—for example, participating in budgeting and shopping experiences, earning and saving an allowance, and playing games involving money concepts—other students might not have these experiences with money. Hence, you should expect that some students may be challenged to learn money in the school context.

You should now return to the money problem in figure 6.1 (page 119). Consider different combinations to make 45¢. What if Jackie had dimes in her purse? The denominations of coins available for the problem make a difference. What if she had three dimes, two nickels, and five pennies? Consider a student who counts by tens first, then fives, and then ones to check to see if the total was 45¢. The student says, "Ten, twenty, thirty, thirty-five, forty, forty-one, forty-two, forty-three, forty-four, forty-five." This student needs to be able to switch from counting by tens to counting by fives to counting by ones in the midst of counting, because the unit would change from a ten to a five to a one. This is a challenging process for young learners.

Problems dealing with money provide opportunities to plan for student engagement in high-cognitive-demand tasks. Tasks should be designed to make connections to other topics beyond measurement and money, such as counting, addition, and subtraction strategies, flexible number representations, and word problem contexts. The task in figure 6.10 (page 130) provides an opportunity for you to review the problem structures from chapter 2 as you write word problems for several problem types.

What money amounts did you use in your word problems? Would the problems involve regrouping? How might students solve them in ways different from how you thought of them while writing them? Anticipating students' responses (both correct and incorrect) to problems can help you write problems with multiple purposes. In what ways did the problems you wrote provide opportunities to uncover common errors?

The Classroom

Now that you have made sense of measurement, think about what instruction looks like when the focus is on developing conceptual understanding with topics related to measurement. The included video links provide opportunities to observe students in action. The first video offers a window into a grade 2 class where students explore how the size of the unit influences the number of units it takes to measure a given object. The second video connects work with measurement to fraction comparison. Grade 3 students are comparing fractions that have common numerators by examining the denominators. You might wonder how this is related to measurement in the primary grades. It will be made explicit in the discussion of the video.

As you watch the first video, take note of how the concept of the inverse relationship between the size of the unit and the number of units it takes to measure an object is developed. Pay attention to how the teacher provides opportunities for the students to do the sense making. Notice the questions that promote student understanding, and watch for a strategy the teacher uses to maintain a high level of student engagement. View the first video before proceeding.

www.solution-tree.com/Measuring
_Length_Using_Different_Units

Now that you have watched the video, think about how learning is supported. Who makes sense of the problem? Who determines if the students' solutions are right or wrong? How are students supported to make sense of each other's thinking?

Write three different word problems that involve combinations of dollar bills, quarters, dimes, nickels, and pennies so that each word problem represents a different problem type in the chart.

		Result Unknown	Change Unknown	Start Unknown
Action	**Join**			
	Separate			
		Whole Unknown		**Part Unknown**	
	Part-Part-Whole			
			Difference Unknown	**Greater Unknown**	**Lesser Unknown**
Nonaction	**Compare**	"How many more?"			
		"How many fewer?"			

Figure 6.10: Writing money problems aligned to the addition and subtraction problem-types chart task.

*Visit **go.solution-tree.com/mathematics** for a free reproducible version of this figure.*

The teacher begins this lesson by directing students to measure the length of the straw. He provides the units to each group but gives no indication that the groups are given units of different lengths from one another. The teacher purposefully selected this task to address the primary goal of the lesson: to engage students in exploring the relationship between the size of the unit and the number of units needed to measure an object. When students share the measures of their straws, the teacher makes sure that students hear that classmates have answers different from their own. He even writes the different answers on the board: 2, 4, and 8. This is an intentional teacher move to create dissonance, and it likely increases the students' engagement with the lesson. They are fairly confident that they are correct because the task itself is not difficult. How could their classmates get it wrong?

This contrived tension is helpful in that the students are now curious to see how their classmates erred. The first student who responds adamantly says, "They were wrong; we were right!" Another student indicates that the other groups must not have checked their answers.

Eventually, a student conjectures that the other groups might be right because their "blocks" could be different. The teacher does not acknowledge if this student is correct but gives the student a block different from the one her group used. The teacher is intentional about not giving the student enough blocks to measure the straw with the new unit. The goal is for the student to reason about measuring with the unit, not to use the unit to measure. The student then reasons that since her group got an answer of four units, the shorter block she is given must have been used to get the answer of eight units. This student is beginning to make sense of the inverse relationship between the size of the unit and the number of units it takes to measure a given object.

Rather than acknowledging the correctness of the student either verbally or through body language, the teacher simply asks others in the class to repeat what she said. Think about the effect of this technique when a student makes sense of a difficult topic. By withholding acknowledgement of correctness and praise for a correct answer at this point, the teacher is opening the conversation to more class members. The other students are given additional opportunities to do the sense making.

The next student who shares provides an excellent explanation that might have been missed if the teacher told the students they were correct. He goes on to provide opportunities for two additional students to share their thinking regarding the inverse relationship in their own words. It is important for students to make sense of this concept, as they will use it in later grades.

The second video extends this same concept in a grade 3 class focused on comparing fractions. Students in this class are comparing fractions with common numerators. The goal is for students to see that if they are comparing the same number of pieces; in this case they are comparing one piece to another single piece, they only need to look at the size of the pieces to determine the greater fraction. Why do you suppose the teacher chose this task? How does the teacher help students make sense of this concept? In what ways does she scaffold instruction? Watch the second video before proceeding.

www.solution-tree.com/Comparing_Fractions
_by_Focusing_on_Numerators

Students are comparing ⅕ and ⅙ to see which is greater. More students in the class have the correct answer of ⅕, but some students have the incorrect answer of ⅙. Rather than selecting a student with the correct answer first, the teacher calls on a student with the incorrect answer to share his thinking. The expectation is that the students who have the correct answer will say they don't agree, since it is a classroom norm to say when one doesn't agree. The expectation is met, and a student explains why the first student is incorrect and helps the student see his error. Later, when the teacher poses a more challenging question, she returns to the student who was originally wrong, having collected and saved this evidence to use beneficially at this point, so that she can check his new understanding and give him an opportunity to share a correct response. She doesn't allow him to explain the entire solution so that others in the class are given the opportunity to do the sense making as well.

The class goes on to use the idea that the more pieces you cut a pizza into, the smaller the pieces. This concept was first developed in second grade when students saw that the smaller the unit, the more units it takes to measure an object. The teacher engages the students in Mathematical Practice 7, "Look for and make use of structure," when the students use this relationship they developed in the first problem—that the more pieces a whole is divided into the smaller the pieces—to solve the second problem where the number of pieces leftover is the same. The teacher also supports student engagement in Mathematical Practice 5, "Use appropriate tools strategically," by providing tools that the students can use to solve the problem but not requiring their use. Some students find the fraction circles helpful in the first problem and go on to use them to make sense of the second problem, but then they see that the tool becomes limited in reaching the solution and are forced to reason without it.

TQE Process

At this point, it may be helpful to watch the first video again (page XX). Pay close attention to the tasks, questioning, and opportunities to collect evidence of student learning.

The TQE process can help you frame your observations. Teachers who have a deep understanding of the mathematics they teach:

- Select appropriate *tasks* to support identified learning goals

- Facilitate productive *questioning* during instruction to engage students in the Mathematical Practices

- Collect and use student *evidence* in the formative assessment process during instruction

The *task* chosen for this lesson supports the students in making a connection between the length of an object and the number of objects needed to measure the straw. The students likely recognize that they are all measuring the length of a straw, but it becomes obvious that they are not aware of the fact that they have different-sized objects with which to measure. The teacher purposefully designed the task to provide the opportunity for the students to experience that it can be possible to measure the same item and arrive at a different number of units. The task effectively creates dissonance in the class so that students see the importance of the size of the unit in measuring. The teacher selected the task in order to guide students to focus on the inverse relationship between the length of the unit and the number of units it takes to measure the object. The task is appropriate to support students to engage in Mathematical Practice 8, "Look for and express regularity in repeated reasoning." He implements it in a way that further supports students in making sense of the measurement concept.

Notice how the teacher uses *questioning* as a way to promote classroom discourse. He provides students the opportunity to do the sense making as they reason about one another's answers and why they are different. The teacher is supporting students to engage in Mathematical Practice 3, "Construct viable arguments and critique the reasoning of others," by withholding the correct answer and directing students to make sense of the multiple answers provided by the class. The teacher provides several opportunities for students to construct the arguments and make sense of one another's reasoning. This is accomplished as a result of the classroom norms in place: students are expected to explain and justify their answers, make sense of each other's answers, and say when they don't understand or don't agree.

The students provide *evidence* of their learning as they participate in the conversation. These important classroom conversations offer the teacher evidence to support the direction of instruction during the lesson as well as in planning future lessons. The teacher begins collecting data by asking students to verify how they determined their answer. Two different students provide correct explanations of their work, giving the teacher evidence of their ability to measure. The teacher then asks how other groups may have determined different answers. With each question, the teacher discovers how the students consider possible alternate approaches to the task. It becomes evident who uses the inverse relationship between the size of the unit and the number of units necessary to measure an object, and the teacher responds appropriately using the formative assessment process throughout the lesson. As the students share their responses, he is able to keep track of this evidence and provide follow-up responses.

The Response

Much of what students struggle with related to measurement links to other areas in mathematics. For example, students with difficulties counting money often also struggle with unitizing. As the coins being counted change, the student needs to keep track of the value of the unit. Students who are still limited to counting exclusively by ones will have difficulty with this process. Focusing on fact strategies and place value supports students, helping them experience more success with counting money. For instance, adding two-digit numbers on the hundred chart as described in chapter 3 might help students change units while counting if students are encouraged to add on the tens and then the ones. Mathematical Practice 6, "Attend to precision," and Mathematical Practice 7, "Look for and make use of structure," are key in addressing these struggles with students.

Other errors students experience with money are identifying and assigning value to coins. Depending on students' experiences outside the classroom, they will have varying levels of comfort with money. Some will recognize coins because they are the same types of coins as the ones in their piggy banks. Others will not have used, or even held, coins outside of school. Students need many opportunities to interact with money models. Pictures of coins are often used in instruction and can be helpful; however, they can also be a hindrance. For example, students cannot move a picture of a dime to place it on top of a picture of a quarter. Hence, students may still have difficulty distinguishing a dime from a quarter. Having access to real coins or model coins can be beneficial to students' learning experiences.

Also be strategic in your planning and instruction related to telling time and linear measurement. As described previously, telling time with an analog clock is a difficult task, since the clock contains many units of measure and symbols containing more than one meaning. Similarly, when engaging with linear measurement, students struggle when transitioning from nonstandard to standard units of measure. This is another example of how attention to supporting student engagement in Mathematical Practice 7, "Look for and make use of structure," is a useful component of the response when students struggle.

Reflections

1. What do you feel are the key points in this chapter?

2. What challenges might you face when implementing the key ideas from this chapter? How will you overcome them?

3. What are the important features for developing an understanding of measurement, and how will you ensure your instruction embeds the support needed for these features?

4. Select a recent lesson focused on measurement that you have taught or observed. Relate this lesson to the TQE process.

5. What changes will you make to your planning and instruction based on what you read and considered from this chapter?

EPILOGUE

Next Steps

An important role of mathematics teachers is to help students understand mathematics as a focused, coherent, and rigorous area of study, regardless of the specific content standards used. To teach mathematics with such depth, you must have a strong understanding of mathematics yourself as well as a myriad of teaching strategies and tools with which to engage students. Hopefully, by providing the necessary knowledge, tools, and opportunities for you to become a *learner* of mathematics once more, this book has empowered you to fill this role.

Now what? How do you take what you learned from *doing* mathematics and make good use of it as the *teacher* of mathematics?

Our position is that you first need to apply what you learned to your lesson planning. Are you planning for instruction that focuses on teaching concepts before procedures? How is your planning aligned to developing learning progressions? How will you ensure that your lessons do not end up as a collection of activities? What follows are strategies that will help you use what you experienced as learners and apply it to what you do as teachers.

Focus on Content

At the heart of meaningful mathematics experiences is mathematics content. A focus on content addresses the *what* of mathematics instruction. What is the mathematical idea or concept you want students to develop and learn as a result of the lesson you facilitate? With your collaborative team, discuss the content that will best serve your students as you progress through the school year. Everything that happens in a mathematics lesson—every task, every activity, every question, every element of the formative assessment process—provides an opportunity to strengthen students' understanding of mathematics content. Thus, it is important for you and your team to engage in collaborative planning about the mathematics content of a unit before the unit begins. Having made sense of mathematics for teaching provides you with a focus on content that will help you and your students have more meaningful and productive experiences with mathematics.

Select Good Tasks

As you've seen throughout this book, your focus on content is revealed in the tasks you select for students to engage in during instruction, so be sure to address this element of instruction during planning. Good tasks are those that support students in learning meaningful mathematics (concepts and, when appropriate, procedures). Other byproducts of good tasks include students engaging in meaningful discourse, developing critical thinking, having multiple ways of representing their thinking (definitions, equations, drawings, and so on), and building fluency (choosing strategies that are most efficient for a given task) in mathematics.

Good tasks also support students in acquiring proficiency with the Mathematical Practices, thereby supporting students' development in mathematics that will last beyond their current grade of study. As you teach, you have the opportunity to engage in the formative assessment process through the use of good tasks. By selecting good tasks, you set the stage for your students to develop strong conceptual understanding of mathematics. We modeled this for you through the tasks provided in this book.

Align Instruction With the Progression of Mathematics

Knowing how mathematics progresses within and across grades is a valuable asset for planning mathematics lessons. As students develop mathematically, you want their classroom experiences to be aligned with how the mathematics should progress. These understandings are important in both planning and implementing instruction processes. In this book, we've facilitated the alignment of instruction with the progression of mathematics within and across grades.

Build Your Mathematics Content Knowledge

Throughout this book, we have addressed mathematics content that is meaningful for your grade band. We have also addressed the content from the perspective that teachers need to facilitate meaningful mathematics instruction. In each chapter, we encouraged you to engage with the mathematics for the purpose of building your mathematics content knowledge by doing mathematics. Our aim was to provide you the support you needed for your understanding of mathematics so that you could subsequently engage your students in similar ways.

Observe Other Teachers of Mathematics

Making Sense of Mathematics for Teaching Grades K–2 has provided you the opportunity to observe mathematics teaching in action. Through videos and examples, you were able to see students engaged in meaningful mathematics based on rich tasks. We hope this provided an opportunity for you to nurture discourse within your collaborative teams about teaching and learning mathematics. For each video, our aim was to guide you to examine the teacher moves and student exchanges that support the students' learning of mathematics. We are confident that each video provides nuggets of insight and confirmation that will help you clarify your thinking about and improve your teaching of mathematics. We encourage you to continue this practice by observing your fellow teachers when possible and inviting them to observe you.

Respond Appropriately to Students' Struggles With Mathematics

Students' progress in mathematics is often met with some level of struggle with understanding mathematics concepts and applying procedures. Some students even struggle with the language (the words, symbols, and so on) of mathematics. Some misunderstandings are unintentionally perpetuated when teachers do not deeply understand mathematics (such as, subtracting always makes smaller, or multiplication always makes larger). By preparing for common misunderstandings and errors, you will be better able to help students successfully engage with mathematics and overcome barriers to understanding. Using the formative assessment process to determine what students know and do not know provides opportunities for you and your collaborative team to reflect together to improve instruction.

Now What?

How has *Making Sense of Mathematics for Teaching Grades K–2* helped prepare you for your next steps? How will you use the TQE process to inform your practice?

- How will you select appropriate *tasks* to support identified learning goals?

- How will you facilitate productive *questioning* during instruction to engage students in the Mathematical Practices?

- How will you collect and use student *evidence* in the formative assessment process during instruction?

In responding to these questions within your collaborative team, your focus should also include the four critical, guiding questions of PLCs (DuFour et al., 2010).

1. What do we want students to learn and be able to do?

2. How will we know if they know it?

3. How will we respond if they don't know it?

4. How will we respond if they do know it?

Now that you have reached the conclusion of this book, we also ask you to respond to these three questions in the spirit of continuing the reflective process.

1. What do you know now that you did not know before interacting with this book?

2. What do you still need to learn now that you have completed this book?

3. How will you obtain the knowledge you still need?

Appendix A:
Completed Classification
of Triangles Chart

	Is always . . .	Is sometimes . . .	Is never . . .
An equilateral triangle	isosceles, acute		scalene, right, obtuse
An isosceles triangle		equilateral, right, acute, obtuse	scalene
A scalene triangle		right, acute, obtuse	equilateral, isosceles
A right triangle		isosceles, scalene	equilateral, acute, obtuse
An acute triangle		equilateral, isosceles, scalene	right, obtuse
An obtuse triangle		scalene, isosceles	equilateral, right, acute

Appendix B: Completed Diagram for Classifying Quadrilaterals

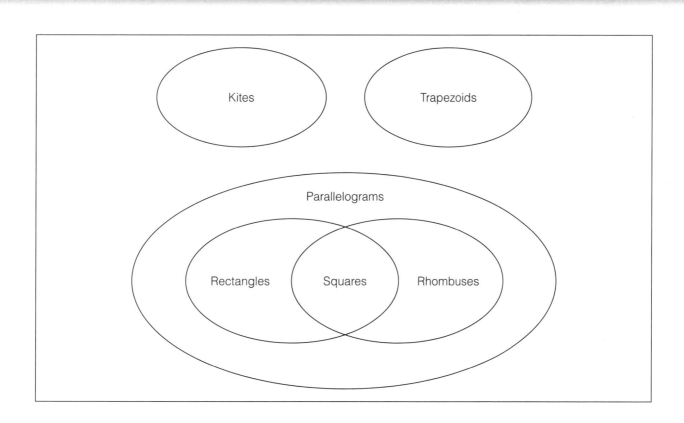

References

Ball, D. L., Thames, M. H., & Phelps, G. (2008). Content knowledge for teaching: What makes it special? *Journal of Teacher Education, 59*(5), 389–407.

Carpenter, T. P., Ansell, E., Franke, M. L., Fennema, E., & Weisbeck, L. (1993). Models of problem solving: A study of kindergarten children's problem-solving processes. *Journal for Research in Mathematics Education, 24*(5), 428–441.

Carpenter, T. P., Fennema, E., Franke, M. L., Levi, L., & Empson, S. B. (2015). *Children's mathematics: Cognitively guided instruction* (2nd ed.). Portsmouth, NH: Heinemann.

Clements, T. B. (2011). *The role of cognitive and metacognitive reading comprehension strategies in the reading and interpretation of mathematical word problem texts: Reading clinicians' perceptions of domain relevance and elementary students' cognitive strategy use* (Unpublished doctoral dissertation). University of Central Florida, Orlando.

Dixon, J. K., Adams, T. L., & Nolan, E. C. (2015). *Beyond the Common Core: A handbook for mathematics in a PLC at Work, grades K–5*. T. D. Kanold (Ed.). Bloomington, IN: Solution Tree Press.

DuFour, R., DuFour, R., Eaker, R., & Many, T. (2010). *Learning by doing: A handbook for Professional Learning Communities at Work* (2nd ed.). Bloomington, IN: Solution Tree Press.

Fisher, D., & Frey, N. (2003). Writing instruction for struggling adolescent readers: A gradual release model. *Journal of Adolescent and Adult Literacy, 46*(5), 396–405.

Karp, K. S., Bush, S. B., & Dougherty, B. J. (2014). 13 rules that expire. *Teaching Children Mathematics, 21*(1), 18–25.

Kilpatrick, J., Swafford, J., & Findell, B. (Eds.). (2001). *Adding it up: Helping children learn mathematics*. Washington, DC: National Academies Press.

Kisa, M. T., & Stein, M. K. (2015). Learning to see teaching in new ways: A foundation for maintaining cognitive demand. *American Educational Research Journal, 52*(1), 105–136.

National Council of Supervisors of Mathematics. (2014). *It's TIME: Themes and imperatives for mathematics education*. Bloomington, IN: Solution Tree Press.

National Council of Teachers of Mathematics. (2000). *Principles and standards for school mathematics*. Reston, VA: Author.

National Council of Teachers of Mathematics. (2014). *Principles to actions: Ensuring mathematical success for all*. Reston, VA: Author.

National Governors Association Center for Best Practices & Council of Chief State School Officers. (2010). *Common Core State Standards for mathematics*. Washington, DC: Authors. Accessed at www.corestandards.org/assets/CCSSI_Math%20Standards.pdf on January 31, 2015.

National Research Council. (2009). *Mathematics learning in early childhood: Paths toward excellence and equity.* Washington, DC: National Academies Press.

Stein, M. K., & Smith, M. S. (1998). Mathematical tasks as a framework for reflection: From research to practice. *Mathematics Teaching in the Middle School, 3*(4), 268–275.

Stigler, J. W., Gonzales, P., Kawanaka, T., Knoll, S., & Serrano, A. (1999). The TIMSS videotape classroom study: Methods and findings from an exploratory research project on eighth-grade mathematics instruction in Germany, Japan, and the United States. *Education Statistics Quarterly, 1*(2), 109–112.

Index

L

layers of facilitation, 10, 21
Levi, L., 31
linear measurement, 123–126

M

make-a-ten strategy, 3, 21, 56, 58
making sense
    conceptual understanding, 2
    of mathematics, 2–6
    procedural skills, 2
    structure of, 6–11
manipulatives, use of, 23–25, 30
Mathematical Practice 1, 46, 55, 66, 98, 101
Mathematical Practice 2, 33, 37, 59
Mathematical Practice 3, 25, 30, 48, 82, 86, 88, 89, 113
Mathematical Practice 4, 39, 63, 66
Mathematical Practice 5, 30, 55, 65
Mathematical Practice 6, 79, 84, 89, 98–99, 101, 109, 112, 114, 117, 133
Mathematical Practice 7, 14, 23, 46, 53, 61, 78, 89, 120, 133
Mathematical Practice 8, 23
mathematical practices, engaging in, 4–5
mathematical proficiency, 4
mathematics, making sense of, 2–6
Mathematics (examples) section, description of, 8–9
measurement
    division, 43
    learning progression, 121–123
    linear, 123–126
    money concepts, 128–129, 130
    student errors, common, 133
    task, geoboard fourths, 125–126
    tasks, 119–121
    telling time, 127–128
    TQE process, 132–133
    videos, 129–133
money

concepts, 128–129, 130
    use of, 24
multidigit addition, 75–79
multidigit subtraction, 64, 83
multiplication word problems, 42–43
Multi-Tiered System of Supports (MTSS), 11

N

National Council of Supervisors of Mathematics (NCSM), 8
number concepts
    defined, 13
    examples, 17–25
    learning progression, 16–17
    student errors, common, 29–30
    task, candy packaging, 13–15, 26–27, 71–73
    TQU process, 27–29
    videos, 25–27
number lines, open, 58, 61–64
number sense, fostering, 20–21

O

one-to-one correspondence, 18
open number lines, 58, 61–64

P

partial sums (break-apart) strategy, 64–65
part-part-whole, 35, 55
pennies, use of, 24
perceptual subitizing, 19
place value
    defined, 13
    examples, 17–25
    focusing on, 23–25
    learning progression, 16–17
    student errors, common, 29–30
    task, candy packaging, 13–15, 26–27, 71–73
    TQU process, 27–29
    videos, 25–27

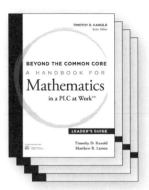

Beyond the Common Core series
Edited by Timothy D. Kanold
Designed to go well beyond the content of your state's standards, this series offers K–12 mathematics instructors and other educators in PLCs an action-oriented guide for focusing curriculum and assessments to positively impact student achievement.
BKF627, BKF628, BKF626, BKF634

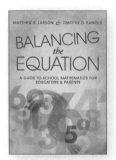

Balancing the Equation
By Matthew R. Larson and Timothy D. Kanold
This book focuses on educators and parents who seek to improve students' understanding and success in mathematics. The authors tackle misconceptions about mathematics education and draw on peer-reviewed research about the instructional elements that can significantly improve student learning.
BKF723

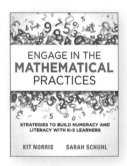

Engage in the Mathematical Practices
By Kit Norris and Sarah Schuhl
Discover more than 40 strategies for ensuring students learn critical reasoning skills and retain understanding. Each chapter is devoted to a different Standard for Mathematical Practice and offers an in-depth look at why the standard is important for students' understanding of mathematics. Grades K–5
BKF670

It's About Time
Edited by Austin Buffum and Mike Mattos
Carve out effective intervention and extension time at all three tiers of the RTI pyramid. Explore more than a dozen examples of creative and flexible scheduling, and gain access to tools you can use immediately to overcome implementation challenges.
BKF609

What We Know About Mathematics Teaching and Learning, Third Edition
By McREL
Designed for accessibility, this book supports mathematics education reform and brings the rich world of education research and practice to pre K–12 educators. It asks important questions, provides background research, offers implications for improving classroom instruction, and lists resources for further reading.
BKF395

Solution Tree | Press
a division of

Solution Tree

Visit solution-tree.com or call 800.733.6786 to order.

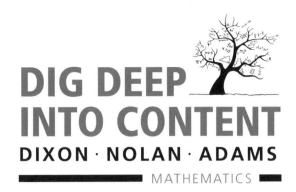

DIG DEEP INTO CONTENT
DIXON · NOLAN · ADAMS
MATHEMATICS

Bring Dixon Nolan Adams Mathematics experts to your school

Juli K. Dixon

Edward C. Nolan

Thomasenia Lott Adams

Janet B. Andreasen
Guy Barmoha
Lisa Brooks
Kristopher Childs
Craig Cullen
Brian Dean

Lakesia L. Dupree
Jennifer Eli
Erhan Selcuk Haciomeroglu
Tashana Howse
Stephanie Luke
Amanda Miller

Samantha Neff
George J. Roy
Farshid Safi
Jennifer Tobias
Taylar Wenzel

Our Services

1. Big-Picture Shifts in Content and Instruction

Introduce content-based strategies to transform teaching and advance learning.

2. Content Institutes

Build the capacity of teachers on important concepts and learning progressions for grades K–2, 3–5, 6–8, and 9–12 based upon the *Making Sense of Mathematics for Teaching* series.

3. Implementation Workshops

Support teachers to apply new strategies gained from Service 2 into instruction using the ten high-leverage team actions from the *Beyond the Common Core* series.

4. On-Site Support

Discover how to unpack learning progressions within and across teacher teams; focus teacher observations and evaluations on moving mathematics instruction forward; and support implementation of a focused, coherent, and rigorous curriculum.

Evidence of Effectiveness

Pasco County School District | Land O' Lakes, FL

Demographics

- 4,937 Teachers
- 68,904 Students
- 52% Free and reduced lunch

Discovery Education Benchmark Assessments

Grade	EOY 2014 % DE	EOY 2015 % DE
2	49%	66%
3	59%	72%
4	63%	70%
5	62%	75%

> "The River Ridge High School Geometry PLC went from ninth out of fourteen high schools in terms of Geometry EOC proficiency in 2013–2014 to first out of fourteen high schools in Pasco County, Florida, for the 2014–2015 school year."
>
> —Katia Clouse, Geometry PLC leader, River Ridge High School, New Port Richey, Florida

Contact your local representative
888.409.1682